BIRTH OF A
NATION

CANADA IN THE 20TH CENTURY
1900 TO 1929

PAUL STANWAY

CanMedia Inc.
Edmonton
2006

Author and Editor
PAUL STANWAY

Layout and Design
DEAN PICKUP

Proofreading
FAITH FARTHING
NICOLE STANWAY

Index
MOIRA CALDER

Published By
CanMedia Inc.

President
CURTIS STEWART

Publisher
RODNEY DIETZMANN

Suite 202,
10479 - 184 Street,
Edmonton, Alberta.
T5S 2L1
Phone (780) 486-6735
Fax (780) 486-6726
Toll Free: 1-888-301-2664
www.cdnhistory.com

Occasionally we make our subscriber list available to carefully screened companies whose products and services might be of interest to our subscribers. If you would like to have your name removed from this list, write to us at the address above.

Printed in Canada
By Friesens Corporation, Altona, Manitoba

BIRTH OF A NATION
CANADA IN THE 20TH CENTURY
1900 - 1929

Birth Of A Nation,
Canada In The 20th Century.
Includes bibliographical references and Index.
ISBN 0-9736530-4-3
ISBN 978-0-9736530-4-5

EAN 9780973653045

1. Canada - History - 1900-1929
11. Stanway, Paul, 1950- .

ISBN 0-9736530-4-3

9 780973 653045

FOREWORD

Purists might argue that this volume is misnamed, since Canada as a country was born in 1867. But as historians and commentators have long noted, Canada's early years were largely an era of unfulfilled potential - as a lack of investment and people slowed settlement and economic growth. In fact, as noted in these pages, some two million Canadians voted with their feet and moved to the United States. All of that changed in the final years of the 19th century, as discoveries of gold in South Africa, the Yukon, and elsewhere provided a new source of capital, ended the global economic recession, and created new demand for Canada's abundant natural resources. In the space of a few short years it turned the young country into an economic tiger and a magnet for immigrants.

It was a common enough belief at the end of the 19th century that the world had reached the limits of its development and was destined to change very little. Thankfully that proved to be far from the truth, and Canada was a major beneficiary of a new era of growth and innovation. The country's image as an Imperial backwater was discarded and the confidence of its people revitalised. In the enthusiastic words of Sir Wilfrid Laurier, Canada had become "the star towards which all men who love progress and freedom shall come." It was the beginning of three tumultuous decades of political, economic and social development that in large measure would determine the nation Canada would become.

This is also the story of the late-Victorian and Edwardian settlers, entrepreneurs, soldiers, and politicians who wielded such a profound influence on the early development of Canada - and whose legacy we live with still. Victorians and Edwardians generally get a bad press these days, portrayed as stiff-necked, predictable, and allergic to change. Yet while there's no doubt they were socially conservative (the worst sin of our age), they were also great innovators, explorers, and builders. In science, economics, and politics, they remade their world. Canadians were often at the forefront of those developments. Indeed, their enthusiasm and drive make their great-grandchildren look timid by comparison.

Sadly, the incredible story contained in these pages is no longer widely taught in Canadian public schools (and in some provinces not at all). A few years ago, when former Alberta premier Peter Lougheed was asked about his chief regret from his years in office, he pointed to the degradation of Canadian history as a subject in the Alberta school curriculum. His answer surprised some people, but should not have. A country that undervalues its history is destined to lose its most valuable legacy: its own story.

This volume is a small attempt to reverse that trend and to tell that story. As the inevitable result of my own background as a reporter, columnist and editor, it is a journalistic history rather than an academic one. I gratefully acknowledge the assistance of researcher James Leech in helping me find my way. My thanks also to Link Byfield and Curtis Stewart, without whom this volume would never have been written or published. The stunning design of the book is all down to graphic artist Dean Pickup, who has the gift of turning a vision into reality. And lastly, my thanks to Ted Barris, Ted Byfield, Pierre Berton, Michael Bliss, Donald Creighton, J.L. Granatstein, James Gray, Laurier LaPierre, Desmond Morton, C.P. Stacey, and the many others who have worked to preserve this nation's remarkable story - and who, knowingly or unknowingly, fuelled my own interest in Canadian history.

Paul Stanway
Edmonton, Alberta.
December 2005.

TABLE OF CONTENTS

The first Canadian Pacific Railway trans-continental passenger train arrives in Vancouver in 1887, after a five-day journey from Montreal. The railway had reached Port Moody, 20 miles east of Vancouver, the previous year, finally linking the country from coast to coast. At the time Vancouver was a rough and ready town, barely five years old. The arrival of the railway signalled an era of phenomenal growth that would eventually make it the largest port on the Pacific coast of North America.

An early tourist (identified only as Miss Priest) surveys Mount Temple and the Bow River valley from a precarious ledge in the Rocky Mountains National Park. Only the third national park in the world, it was established in 1887 and by 1900 was visited by 8,000 well-heeled travellers from across Canada, the U.S., and Europe. Much enlarged, it would later be renamed Banff National Park.

Glenbow Archives

The Sleeping Giant

A Rocky Beginning To Nationhood
As Two Million Vote With Their Feet

What *is in progress in Canada during the opening years of the 20th century is not the normal growth of a settled community, but the rapid, almost the sudden, economic appropriation of a new land.... The present inhabitants of Canada are a race of conquerors!*

Sidney Webb

When Sidney Webb, the British author and social reformer, wrote those words at the beginning of the 20th century, Canada was a booming economic tiger, the fastest growing economy on earth. What in later times would have been dubbed an economic miracle was changing international perceptions of Canada, and the perceptions Canadians had of themselves. Yet the most remarkable thing about this change was how quickly it had happened.

For most of the last half of the 19th century the country had been regarded as an economic backwater: a land of great but unfulfilled promise, the poor cousin of the great republic to the South. The changing fortune of the Dominion of Canada is one of the great stories of the end of the Victorian era, and one that grasped the imagination of millions. It is also a surprising and, some might say, improbable tale.

The early years of Confederation had not been kind to Canada. Compared to the rapid development and prosperity of its southern neighbour, the Dominion seemed stuck in first gear. From the outset Canada had been an unlikely creation. In the words of the *Acadian Recorder* newspaper in 1867: "We don't know each other. We have no trade with each other. We have no facilities or resources or incentives to mingle with each other. We are shut off from each other by a wilderness, geographically, commercially, politically and socially." It was a pessimistic but accurate description of the new nation, and one which would change only slowly at first.

As the 19th century drew to a close, Canadians did not have a unified idea of who or what they were. Most identified themselves, first and foremost, as English, French, Irish or Scots,

In the last quarter of the 19th century Canada was still a mostly rural country, about to be thrust into the economic limelight. Quebec City (top left) boasted one of the new, electric-powered tramways that were rapidly changing urban transportation in the larger cities. The traffic making its way down Main Street, Lunenburg, Nova Scotia (bottom left), is horse-drawn, but utility poles are already in evidence. For most Canadians however, such as this fisherman and his young helper at Cap-a-l'Aigle, Quebec (below), life at the end of the Victorian era remained quiet and blissfully unhurried.

Photos - National Archives of Canada

Protestant or Catholic, and then perhaps as Nova Scotians, Quebeckers or Ontarians. Cultural, religious and regional differences ran deep, and it often seemed as if the various groups barely tolerated each other. Canada was a country of major contradictions. Its people were subjects of an ancient monarchy and the greatest empire in modern history, yet citizens of a fledgling nation barely 30 years old. It was a land of rugged frontiersmen, dashing Mounties and pioneering farmers, yet also one where more and more people earned their livelihood as factory workers, ticket collectors and bank clerks.

Canada was in many ways a modern country. All the amazing innovations of late-Victorian science and technology - electricity, telephones, streetcars and the first automobiles - could be found in its growing towns and cities, yet beyond these populated areas, still relatively few, there remained a vast and mostly untouched wilderness. The country's potential was obvious, yet largely unrealized. Particularly if you compared it to the United States, which many people did.

During a visit in 1888, the German industrialist Friedrich Engels (patron of Karl Marx) noted: "It is a strange transition from the States to Canada. First one imagines that one is in Europe again, and then one thinks one is in a positively retrogressing and decaying country. Here one sees

Horses hauling a barge on the Market Slip in Saint John, New Brunswick (left) at the beginning of the 20th century. Cheap and reliable, horse power and sail remained the backbone of transportation in many parts of the country, but both were being steadily replaced by steam and the internal combustion engine as Canada's fledgling industrialization gathered speed. The steady shift of economic activity and people to central Canada and the West had serious consequences for bustling east coast ports like Saint John.

National Archives of Canada

how necessary the feverish speculative spirit of the Americans is for the rapid development of a new country; and in 10 years this sleepy Canada will be ripe for annexation."

In an age of enthusiastic imperialism, few Canadians would have agreed with Engels' prediction of early annexation (the country had been created, in large part, to avert that possibility), but they were acutely aware they were less well off than most Americans. They would have been surprised to learn they were less prosperous than Australians or even Argentinians. The most serious and prolonged global economic depression of the 19th century had effectively stalled growth and prosperity. Unemployment and hardship were widespread, and there had been food riots in some cities. The early years of Confederation had been difficult, to say the least, and a test of faith for even the staunchest supporters of the new country.

A union of the colonies of British North America had been talked about for years, but it was the fear of American expansionism in the wake of the Civil War which eventually brought a majority of those colonies together for mutual protection and, they hoped, greater prosperity.

In 1865, as the American Civil War ended, official relations between British North America

An idyllic late Victorian scene (above) of horse-drawn sleighs making their way along Sherbrooke Street, Montreal in the winter of 1896. A quiet village road at Murray Bay, Quebec (top right), and the annual summer horse fair at Galt, Ontario (bottom right). The barely 30-year-old country remained overwhelmingly rural, causing visiting German industrialist Friedrich Engels (mentor of Karl Marx) to comment that "sleepy Canada" was ripe for annexation by its hustling, bustling neighbour to south.

and the United States were at a low ebb. In Britain and its North American colonies (filled with the descendants of the Empire Loyalists), there was no great fondness for the Union and there had been some sympathy for the rebel cause. For its part, the United States was still a country under arms and there was much loose talk of finishing the work of the Revolution and creating one nation on the North American continent. As the *New York Times* reminded its readers: "We were never in better condition for war with England."

Members of the American wing of the Irish Republican Brotherhood, the Fenians, had their own reasons for provoking war with the Canadian colonies. Staunch enemies of the Empire, they saw the conquest of British North America as a first step towards independence for Ireland itself. So while the government in Washington looked the other way, a group of Irish-American officers led by Maj. Gen. Thomas W. Sweeny combed the demobilizing Union army for volunteers for service with the Fenian military wing - the Irish Republican Army (IRA). By the end of May 1866, 5,000 IRA troops had gathered at Buffalo, N.Y. and an ambitious plan of conquest developed.

Too ambitious, as it turned out.

There is still some disagreement about how many IRA troops actually crossed the Niagara River into Ontario (between 600 and 1,500), but they proclaimed a new Republic of Canada, roamed about the Niagara peninsula unchecked for two days and at the Battle of Ridgeway (near Fort Erie) managed to inflict a humiliating defeat on a force of Canadian militia and British regular soldiers. However, denied official recognition by the U.S. government, and not finding

The last years of the 19th century were a time of enormous technological innovation. This winter scene at Niagara-on-the-Lake, Ontario (below) shows a rotary snow plough being used to clear the way for two street cars. The new electric tramways, the country's first mass transit systems, revolutionized urban travel in Canada's towns and cities.

National Archives of Canada

These immigrants at Quebec City are waiting for the mandatory medical before being admitted to the country. Immigration had begun to pick up by the end of the 19th century, but in the years between 1881 and 1901 two million people voted with their feet and left Canada for the U.S. - many of them recent arrivals. Unemployment and hardship were widespread until the mid-1890s, with food riots in some cities.

the expected popular support among Canada's large Irish population, the IRA force eventually retreated across the river.

Not wanting a full-blown confrontation with Britain, within days Washington moved to curb the activities of the Fenians, but the group remained a potential threat to Canada for several years and the inability to effectively defend against even such a disorganized invasion provided the necessary incentive for the creation of a union of the colonies of British North America. The result, in 1867, was Confederation.

The new country - comprised of Ontario, Quebec, New Brunswick and Nova Scotia - had a population of one million French Canadians, 800,000 Irish, 700,000 English, 500,000 Scots, and 200,000 Germans. In addition to Canada (the name by which the two largest provinces had long been known), among the more fanciful names suggested for the new Dominion were Laurentia, New Britain, Cabotia, Ursalia, Borealia, Hochelaga, Tuponia, Colonia and Efisga (an acronym for England, France, Ireland, Scotland, Germany and the aboriginal peoples). D'Arcy McGee, the politician and noted orator, was appalled and challenged those proposing such outlandish suggestions: "How would he feel if he woke up some fine morning and found himself, instead of a Canadian, a Tuponian or a Hochelagander?"

Thankfully, common sense prevailed.

By 1900 Ontario was developing rapidly as Canada's manufacturing centre, but with more farmland (and more people to feed) than any other province, agriculture remained the major industry. Market gardens such as this one (below) near Pembroke supplied growing cities such as Toronto with all manner of fresh produce. Farming in the late Victorian era remained labour intensive, as is made clear in this photograph (opposite page) of a farmer sorting seed corn by hand - just as his father and grandfather might have done.

National Archives of Canada

Canada came into being without much public debate or great fanfare, and even among Confederation's supporters the early decades proved a disappointment. In the 1870s the new country fell into a prolonged economic depression which affected the whole of Europe and North America. Export markets for Canadian goods (mostly agricultural produce) dried up and the small, emerging industries of the Dominion were either snuffed out or seriously damaged. An estimated 10,000 businesses went under. Unemployment and hunger were the rule among working people in the country's towns and cities and desperate farmers in the thousands left the land. There were food riots in Ottawa, Montreal and Kingston and many unhappy Canadians left for greater opportunities in the United States.

The generation born after 1867 had a sense of Canada's potential, but also a clear understanding that this potential was being only slowly exploited. The population increased from 3.3 million in 1867 to 5.3 million in 1900, but that paled against growth in the U.S. over the same period - from 40 million to 75 million! Then as now, the lure of the U.S. was ever-present. Over the two decades from 1881 to 1901 two million people left for the U.S. Some were recent immigrants, but

Two children (below) gaze out over the St. Lawrence River at Cacouna, Quebec. By later standards they seem a little overdressed for digging in the sand, but many Victorian parents were careful about their children's overexposure to the sun. A century later their great-grandchildren would rediscover that concern.

National Archives of Canada

In the later years of the 19th century Ontario still relied heavily on sailing ships to move the province's manufactured goods and agricultural produce around the Great Lakes, and along the St. Lawrence. This photograph (above) shows vessels lined up at the Port Dalhousie locks on the old Welland Ship Canal.

many were Canadians who had given up waiting for the prosperity which always seemed just out of reach. Almost everyone had friends and relatives in the U.S. and in many border areas, from New England to Michigan, transplanted Canadians made up a majority of the population.

As the explorer Jacques Cartier had first noted in 1534, Canada often appeared to be "the land God gave to Cain." A popular joke of the early 1890s held that the only parts of the *Old Testament* which effectively described Canada were *Lamentations* and *Exodus*. The opportunities south of the border seemed, and often were, greater. What later generations would call the "brain drain" was at this time more general: a veritable population drain. It served to starve Canada of many energetic, younger citizens who went south to find what they could not find at home.

In the late 1880s there was a brief economic upswing based on increased timber exports and the railway boom, but it didn't last. Even in the new lands of the West, farmers abandoned homesteads in alarming numbers. According to North-West Mounted Police Commissioner Lawrence Herschmer, "some districts that were once well settled now are deserted, and in others there are only two or three settlers left."

The country struggled on under the charismatic and determined leadership of its first prime minister, Sir John A. Macdonald. A deft and shrewd politician, Macdonald's ability to manage the conflicting religious, cultural and regional interests which made up the new Dominion gave him an almost mythical reputation and usually allowed him to fend off challenges from those who didn't share his single-minded devotion to the idea of Canada. Even the main political opponent of his later years, Liberal leader Wilfrid Laurier, lauded the hard-drinking Macdonald for his "far reaching vision beyond the event of the day, and still higher, permeating the whole, a broad patriotism, a devotion to Canada's welfare, Canada's advancement, Canada's glory."

What, exactly, was the Canada to which Macdonald and Laurier were so devoted?

Nova Scotia, New Brunswick and Prince Edward Island (which entered Confederation in 1873) had deep traditions of provincial loyalty and a strong sense of identity. Under the protective tariffs of the Macdonald government's National Policy, Nova Scotia in particular prospered in the closing decades of the 19th century. The arrival of new railway lines dramatically improved connections to the vast hinterland of North America, and Truro, New Glasgow, Amherst and Sidney found new markets for their coal and steel. But it was a short-lived boom. Resources were being developed which were closer to the new industrial centres around the Great Lakes. Halifax remained the headquarters for the North American squadron of the Royal Navy and a major port. But already the Maritimes' main contribution to the new country was people. From all walks of life, they left in their thousands to help populate the expanding cities of southern Ontario and the empty West. In particular they became the backbone of the army of teachers who fanned out over the country to educate a generation of newcomers.

The woman in white in this photo (above) of two Edwardian ladies out for a stroll near Cantley, Quebec, is holding a Kodak No. 1 Folding Pocket Camera. One of the first mass-produced cameras designed specifically for amateurs to take snapshots, the Kodak No. 1 was popular with the growing number of middle-class leisure travellers.

An outing by motor boat on Portage Bay in Ontario's Muskoka Lakes (below). The area was already becoming a popular destination for visitors and cottagers - and not only from Ontario. The Stars and Stripes adorning the boat suggests these may have been Americans.

Quebeckers, as always, differentiated themselves on linguistic and religious lines, but by the end of the 19th century there were other sharp divisions developing between urban and rural Quebec. Anglophones were becoming predominantly city dwellers, while *les Canadiens* were encouraged by church and civic leaders to stay on the land. Montreal was the largest city in the country and home to most of Canada's business leaders and millionaires. It boasted 320 kilometres of paved streets and a number of the noisy new automobiles (although an estimated 2,800 stables confirmed the continuing reliance on traditional horsepower). Older Quebec City remained resolutely French, despite a substantial Irish minority in the suburb of Sillery, and was home to the francophone political elite who governed the province. Quebeckers with itchy feet tended to look south to the U.S. rather than to the Canadian West, and some half a million moved to New England in the 1870s and 80s. There were even some (Honore Mercier, the provincial Liberal leader among them) who thought Quebec would be better off as an American state.

Ontario was still a predominantly agricultural province. Though smaller in area than Quebec, it boasted more fertile farmland and had by the middle of the 19th century surpassed its eastern neighbour in population. Sober and sensible Toronto, by now the largest city in the province, was considerably smaller than Montreal and lagged far behind its rival in large private homes and lavish public monuments. It had fewer paved streets, one automobile (owned by a member of the Massey family) and

had been bypassed as a major rail terminus. Yet by 1900 the city was already home to a substantial manufacturing industry, producing everything from chocolates to pianos to agricultural implements for a growing national market. The demand for investment meant it was rapidly developing its own financial sector. Ottawa had benefited from its status as the national capital, and government had already joined agriculture, timber and the railway as a major contributor to the city's prosperity. Hamilton was home to a growing steel industry, which benefited from the same subsidies and tax incentives used in Cape Breton, but it had the advantage of being located in a region which was becoming the industrial heartland of North America. Kingston, London, St. Catharines and other market towns across southern Ontario had developed into significant regional centres.

Over the next few decades Canada's westward expansion and the growth of the province's manufacturing sector would transform Ontario into a supplier of just about everything the new wave of immigrants would need to bring the West under the plough and establish thriving cities of their own. If the 18th and 19th centuries had belonged to Quebec and Montreal, the 20th century would belong to southern Ontario and in particular Toronto, transforming it into the largest, most prosperous and most powerful city in the country.

Manitoba had joined Confederation in 1870 and was very much the child of Ontario. The arrival of the railroad had brought the province dramatically closer to Canada's heartland and a wave of settlement from Ontario had transformed its frontier society. The rapid changes were—

An elderly knife sharpener plying his trade on the streets of Toronto (opposite page). With little in the way of social assistance, self-reliance was a necessity at the end of the Victorian era and many people eked out a living by offering services on the street or selling their own produce door to door. For the younger and more adventurous, the sparsely populated West beckoned. Not all were successful. Saskatchewan's Barr Colonists (below, unloading supplies at Saskatoon) foundered in their attempt to establish a little piece of Britain on the Canadian Prairies.

National Archives of Canada

resisted by Metis and native tribes, who had so recently been the majority, but after a brief power struggle and unsuccessful armed rebellions (in 1869 and again in 1885) it was clear that Manitoba would be the beachhead for colonization of the Canadian Prairies and the template for their development. Winnipeg was rapidly becoming a rail and distribution centre to rival Chicago and was the jumping-off point for thousands (soon to become hundreds of thousands) of European immigrants. That process would transform Manitoba (and eventually the rest of the Canadian West) into a society which was neither English nor French but a new branch of the Canadian family which would, in a remarkably short time, develop its own culture and a new perspective on national issues.

The Northwest Territories, the southern portion of which would soon become Saskatchewan and Alberta, were still sparsely populated lands of apparently limitless opportunity. Ottawa had bought the land from the Hudson's Bay Company for $1.5 million, the greatest real estate bargain in history. Agriculture would be the engine which powered its development, but it was already understood that beneath the western Prairies and the foothills of the Rockies lay perhaps substantial deposits of coal and other resources. Among the people of the Territories there was already developing a sense of shared experience and identity (a reverence for the "pioneer spirit" and a defiant optimism) which would bind westerners together. Canadians are nothing if not intensely regional, and the people of this new region would prove to be no less Canadian in that regard. In the words of Frederick Haultain, the premier who guided the Territories to responsible government, "What we want in the West, and what we have a right to expect, is to be established as a province with equal rights with the rest of the Dominion. We do not ask more, and we will not be willing to take less."

There were settlers and cowboys, miners and prospectors, and a substantial aboriginal population. There were gunfights in the streets of Calgary, rustling and bank holdups. It was raw and it was rugged - yet this was not the Wild West. Government and the rule of law had arrived with the first wagons and Macdonald's legendary paramilitary police force, the North-West Mounted Police (established in 1873). The Mounties were a Canadian original, a unique amalgam of soldier, policeman and magistrate able to dispense justice on the spot - which they did with a combination of toughness and diplomacy which won the force wide respect. As befitted the frontier of a great Dominion and empire, settlement would be accomplished in an orderly fashion.

A lieutenant governor in the territorial capital of Regina (population 2,200) represented Ottawa and the Crown, and a legislature of 35 members represented the Territories' 165,000 residents.

In 1870 Winnipeg's Main Street (below) was typical of a raw western town. You knew you were on the edge of civilization. Less than two decades later, a panoramic photo taken from the roof of the City Hall (opposite page) shows a sprawling, budding metropolis with its first utility poles carrying power and telephone cables. Winnipeg was rapidly becoming a rail and distribution centre to rival Chicago, and would be the jumping off point for many of the European immigrants filling Canada's prairies.

Photos - National Archives of Canada

The largest community was not Calgary (4,000) or Edmonton (2,600), but the booming capital of the Yukon goldfields, Dawson City (9,000).

Beyond the Rocky Mountains, British Columbia's focus was the Pacific and it already saw itself as a land apart. When the province joined Canada in 1871 its representatives made the journey to Ottawa via San Francisco and Chicago. The Canadian Pacific finally linked the province's 180,000 citizens to the rest of the country in the summer of 1886 (five years later than promised), but Ottawa and national concerns still seemed a very long way off. The province boasted enormous resources of timber and minerals - but it would take investment and people to develop them. The Americans had the money and the readiest source of immigration was across the Pacific in Asia, but among B.C.'s small and devoutly British population the fear of being overwhelmed was omnipresent.

Government and the company town would loom large in the province's development (Sir James Dunsmuir was both premier and the province's largest private employer), as would the power of organized labour - creating a polarized political landscape. Vancouver and Victoria were raw, bustling ports built in a hurry to provide a Pacific outlet for the export of natural resources. There was, as yet, no inkling that they would one day be considered among the most attractive places in the entire world in which to live.

As late as the mid-1890s the hoped-for development of Canada's vast western territories remained largely unfulfilled. There were fewer than 350,000 settlers from the Ontario border to the Pacific, joining a native population of about 100,000. Yet it is hard to exaggerate the hold the West had on the imagination of Canadians at the end of the 19th century. While Canada was part of a larger British Empire, the country possessed a western empire of its own: A vast territory as large as Europe, with the tantalizing potential to turn Canada into a wealthy and powerful nation in its own right.

This empty land was supposed to be a magnet for immigration, and the arrival of the railway

By the last years of the 19th century the railways had finally begun to open up the vast North West Territories for settlement, but this was still very much the frontier. In May 1899, outside Edmonton's Alberta Hotel (right), a Treaty Commission party assembles with its North West Mounted Police escort, ready to embark on negotiations with the Territories' native people. Already more than a century old, Edmonton continued to be a centre of the fur trade. On the banks of the North Saskatchewan River (above), near the site of the original trading post, a group of trappers load their gear for a season in the bush.

had increased the pace of settlement. But too many immigrants stayed only briefly before moving on to milder climes and better prospects in the United States. Migration to the U.S. actually increased at the end of the 19th century as the disillusioned packed their belongings and left - among them an astonishing 40 per cent of the farmers in the fledgling province of Manitoba.

Yet things were changing. The young country had brought Manitoba, British Columbia and Prince Edward Island into Confederation and absorbed the vast Hudson's Bay Company holdings (the largest peaceful annexation of land in world history). There was already talk of provincial status for the western Prairies.

The Intercolonial Railway in the East (linking St. John and Halifax with Montreal) and the Canadian Pacific Railway in the West had begun the conquest of the vast distances which had traditionally separated Canadians. The journey from Montreal to Port Vancouver now took five and a half days, whereas previously it had taken months. The old economy of subsistence farming, fishing and the provision of resources for mainly local markets was giving way to an export economy which could take advantage of new developments in transportation, farming and mining, and of innovations such as electricity. Manitoba wheat was already talked of in Britain as the best in the world, which hinted at the enormous export markets to come. All that was needed was capital and people, and the country's great potential might at last be unlocked.

The Banff Springs Hotel at the turn of the last century. The hotel was still a mostly wooden structure, but the arrival of the railway and the creation of Canada's first national park (in 1887) had already turned Banff into an internationally famous destination which attracted visitors from the United States and Europe, as well as wealthy Canadians from the East. The town was named for the Scottish birthplace of Canadian Pacific Railway co-founder Donald Smith, Lord Strathcona, and would never quite lose its Highland flavour.

It is often said that, for Canada, the 20th century actually began in 1896, with revitalized leadership, a resurgent economy and - for the first time in the country's short history - a burst of optimism. The Conservatives, led by Sir Mackenzie Bowell, went down to defeat in the general election of that year. The end of Canada's first political dynasty is usually attributed to Bowell's defence of the education rights of Manitoba's French Catholic minority. Wilfrid Laurier, the Liberal leader, neatly dodged the issue by arguing that a government at the end of its mandate had no right to decide such important matters. Laurier vowed, if elected, to resolve the issue through compromise and "sunny ways."

Quebec voted for its native son in a landslide and even Ontario, supposedly a bastion of belligerent, Protestant conservatism, gave the francophone, Catholic, Liberal Laurier 43 of its 92 seats. Manitobans, ironically, ignored Bowell's supposedly controversial intrusion into provincial education policy and returned a majority of Conservatives!

For the Liberals, it was a timely win. The improving economic outlook offered opportunities for a new government with an energetic new leader and new ideas. Or at least, old ideas reshaped. Laurier, like Macdonald, was a passionate Canadian and an enthusiastic nation-builder. He was a great admirer of the Empire, but he also believed it was Canada's destiny to be a fully independent nation.

The last two decades of the 19th century were a disaster for the native people of the West. The land was no longer theirs, the eternal abundance of the buffalo had gone and a proud, self-reliant people had become wards of a government bureaucracy. At Shaganappi Point outside Calgary (below), this group of native people are gathered to mark a visit by the Duke of York. Calgary's growth at the end of the 19th century was, in some ways, more astonishing than Winnipeg's. In 1886 (right) it was little more than a North West Mounted Police fort and a few businesses supplying the region's ranchers. By the 1890s it was a Canadian Pacific Railway maintenance centre and a substantial town of 4,000 people.

National Archives of Canada

He described his vision this way: "My object is to consolidate Confederation and to bring our people, long estranged from each other, gradually to become a nation. This is the supreme issue. Everything else is subordinate to that idea."

It was hardly a new idea. The cultural, regional and economic challenges facing the country had been recognized and debated from the outset. Historian Goldwin Smith had hit the nail on the head in 1886: "Whether... the Dominion can forever be kept by political agencies united among themselves and separate from their continent, of which geographically, economically and - with the exception of Quebec - culturally they are part, is the Canadian question."

In his attempts to define this new national identity, Laurier would try to follow a path which was not specifically French or English, Catholic or Protestant (the labels which had traditionally defined Canadian voters), and as a result he was often criticized by partisans from all those groups. Like Macdonald before him he was branded a compromiser and arch-conciliator, which he certainly was, but his popularity lay in the fact he never lost sight of his "supreme issue" and for fifteen years was recognized by most Canadians as a unifying force in public life.

Laurier's government was the lucky beneficiary of an economy which was finally starting to live up to its potential. The combination of an unprecedented rate of economic growth, immigration and the harnessing of a host of innovations - from electricity and the telephone to the typewriter and Marquis wheat - would transform Canada from a colonial backwater into an ascendant nation state and an influential voice within the most powerful Empire in the world.

The first train load of ore from the La Roi gold mine (above) in Rossland, British Columbia, 1901. The railway at last made possible the exploitation of B.C.'s rugged, resource-rich interior. At the end of the 19th century prospectors also flooded through the coastal mountains into the Yukon in search of gold, and made Dawson City (opposite page, top) the largest community in the North West Territories - with almost 25,000 inhabitants. The harbour at Nanaimo, B.C. (opposite page, bottom) in 1906. Sailing vessels still predominated, but newer, faster steam ships were beginning to link Canada's Pacific coast with vast overseas markets.

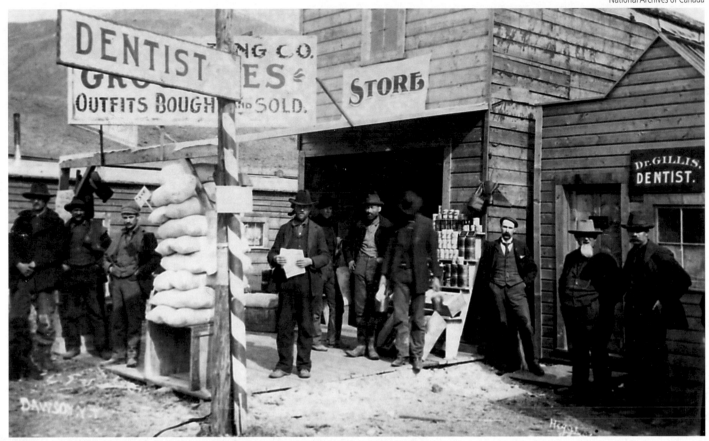

Wilfrid Laurier

The Passionate Compromiser

Canada's first francophone prime minister was born on November 20, 1841, in the village of Saint-Lin, Canada East, less than a year after the merger of Upper and Lower Canada. As a youthful Quebec nationalist, Laurier was opposed to that merger as well as the whole notion of Confederation. But his opposition to the idea of Canada had disappeared by the time he graduated from McGill University in 1864, when he gave a passionate valedictory speech in praise of Canadian unity. "It is to our glory that race hatreds have ended on Canadian soil. There is no longer any family here but the human family. It matters not what language the people speak or at which altars they kneel.... There is glory in this fraternity of which Canada can never be proud enough." The difficulty of governing that "fraternity" would eventually blunt Laurier's youthful idealism, but he would remain a champion of unity and a passionate Canadian.

When he was elected Liberal leader in 1887 few people, even within his own party, thought a French Catholic was the man to break the electoral stranglehold of Sir John A. Macdonald and the Conservatives. Yet after Macdonald died this tall, laconic Victorian gentleman would captivate Canadians and in 1896 lead his party to victory.

Laurier had the knack of making Canadians feel good about themselves and their country at a time of growing national confidence. He was the voice of optimism. His speeches seem theatrical and overblown to the modern reader, but his belief in his country shines through. In a typical speech in Montreal in 1901 he explained: "I love my country because it resembles no other. I love my country because... it calls forth the noblest resolutions, the strongest, the most generous qualities of man. I love my country above all because it is unique in the world, because it is founded on respect for rights, on pride of origin, on harmony and concord between the races who inhabit it.... Let us have in view only the development, the prosperity, the grandeur of our country. Let us keep in our heart this thought: Canada first, Canada forever, nothing but Canada."

The urbane and always impeccably dressed Laurier exuded what later generations would have called charisma. He clearly had a special attraction for women, yet through his long career he managed to avoid the taint of scandal - except for one curious rumour concerning Armand Lavergne, the son of Laurier's law partner. The young man bore a slight resemblance to Laurier, and it was whispered that the prime minister was his father.

Laurier's friendship with Lavergne's mother, Emilie, is well documented (she is credited with helping him polish his manners and dress sense), but whether it was more than platonic is still hotly debated by biographers. What is not in question is that Armand Lavergne did not share Laurier's political vision. With Laurier's encouragement, he served as an MP from 1904 until 1908-but was a constant thorn in his mentor's side. He was said to be so anti-English as to be an out and out racist. Lavergne eventually left federal politics for the Quebec legislature, and was not much heard of after that.

Laurier's popularity and success as a leader remain unmatched, yet his final election, in 1911, created so much bitterness and division it almost destroyed the Liberal party. By then approaching 70, Laurier was accused of selling out the country to the Americans in a proposed free trade deal. He ran on his record and reputation and issued a typical Laurier appeal for unity and compromise: "I have had before me... a policy of true Canadianism, of moderation, of conciliation. I have followed it consistently since 1896, and I now appeal with confidence to the whole Canadian people to uphold me in this policy of sound Canadianism which makes for the greatness of our country and of the Empire."

For the first time since1896 the voters didn't respond, and Laurier spent the rest of his political career in opposition. During

National Archives of Canada

Wilfrid Laurier in 1897, a year after becoming Canada's first francophone and Catholic prime minister. The 1896 election marked the beginning of an era of expansion and prosperity, which boosted the popularity of Laurier's Liberal government.

Zoe Laurier in 1905, looking every inch the elegant Edwardian lady.

Laurier's drive and his vision of a prosperous, populous and independent Canada had a profound impact on the country he loved so passionately. In 1911 there were 7.2 million people in Canada, two million more than when he took office fifteen years earlier. It had become a rapidly developing economic tiger, with $400 million in exports and a robust balance of trade.

Under his leadership the West had begun to realize the potential which thus far had been a dream. He shepherded Canada from the status of a colony with little control over its foreign affairs to that of an influential, senior dominion within the Empire, and a country with the confidence to determine and pursue its own best interests. He promoted an image of Canada as a nation of compassion, respect, moderation and conciliation - which wasn't always true but would be embraced by future governments and would come to form the core of an elusive national identity. ∎

the Great War he refused to join the coalition government of Sir Robert Borden but supported the war effort and continued to use his considerable influence in Quebec to promote national unity. In February 1919, the 78-year-old Laurier suffered a stroke while dressing for church and died the following night. His last words to his wife, Lady Zoe, were "C'est fini."

Laurier's influence was enormous and lasting. He identified the middle ground of Canadian politics and positioned the Liberals as the party of national unity. He created a template for Canadian leadership in which compromise became an end in itself: the Canadian way. He also established the Liberals as the federal voice of Quebec, and in doing so set the pattern of national government for much of the century to come.

Laurier was also an enthusiastic distributor of patronage and preferment and saw those things as necessary tools for effective political leadership and success at the ballot box. In that, too, the most successful of all Canadian prime ministers would leave his mark on Canadian politics.

Above all, Laurier saw himself as a practical politician. Late in his life he wrote that, in politics, it was seldom possible to do the ideal thing. "The best that can be done is to obtain a certain object, and for the accomplishment of this object many things have to be done which are questionable, and many things have to be submitted to which, if vigorously investigated, could not be approved of." It was a creed which would be followed by most, if not all, subsequent prime ministers.

Armand Lavergne, whose superficial resemblance to the prime minister prompted some to suggest the young man might be Laurier's illegitimate offspring with the wife of his law partner.

embership of the Empire framed all of Canada's relations with the outside world. The country could not sign treaties on its own behalf and the prime minister was forced to rely on the governor-general for briefings on foreign policy and political news from around the world. A British officer commanded what passed for a Canadian army, and the Royal Navy patrolled the country's shores. Halifax and Victoria were still home to British garrisons.

This was the Age of Imperialism. Around the world British power was supreme and Queen Victoria's Diamond Jubilee in 1897 had prompted a great surge of imperial pride. Most Canadians of British extraction, the majority, felt very much a part of what was viewed as a huge and noble enterprise and took both comfort and confidence from the imperial connection. Canada was most definitely a junior partner within the Empire, yet the Dominion was beginning to flex its muscles in its relations with Britain - and meeting with some success.

Britain's energetic new colonial secretary, Joseph Chamberlain, pushed for greater coordination and centralization aimed at making the most of the Empire's unparalleled economic and military strength. Canada, with its vast mineral and agricultural potential, was seen as a key component of this imperial vision, but Canada was a self-governing Dominion with ideas of its own. Prime Minister Wilfrid Laurier's goal was to develop among Canadians a common identity and to be treated by Britain as a partner in imperial affairs. This brought Ottawa into direct conflict with Chamberlain's notion of an imperial union more tightly controlled by Britain, but Laurier was a skilful statesman and he gradually succeeded in negotiating better economic links with the Empire without sacrificing Canadian independence.

Relations with London were of supreme importance - most of the capital to finance the country's growth would continue to come from Britain until well into the new century - but the U.S. was already becoming Canada's most important trading partner and Laurier began discussions with Washington on better commercial relations. In a series of meetings in Quebec City and

Gold had first been discovered in the Yukon River valley in 1878, but it wasn't until 1896 that an American, George Washington Carmack, and two Tagish Indians, Skookum Jim and Tagish Charlie, found the precious metal in commercial quantities on a tributary of the Klondike River they named Bonanza Creek. It was estimated that every claim on the creek was worth in excess of $500,000, and within a month thousands of prospectors were trekking over the mountains from the Pacific coast and lining up to register their own claims (below). For the majority of prospectors, the Klondike meant hard work, rough living, and only the rumour of wealth. Yet in three years almost $100 million worth of Yukon gold found its way to the U.S. Treasury vaults at Fort Knox.

At the height of the Klondike gold rush Dawson City boasted all manner of delights - legal and otherwise - including entertainment by the redoubtable Snake Hips Lulu (shown here in a photo taken in 1898), one of the town's most celebrated dance hall queens. Dawson was a wild town, to be sure, but the North West Mounted Police detachment - nine officers and a cook - ensured there was surprisingly little serious crime or disorder.

Washington during 1898 and 1899, Canadian, British and American trade representatives met to discuss the Atlantic and Pacific fisheries and trade in general.

At these meetings, Canada's new self-confidence and determination to put Canadian interests first pleased neither the American nor the British diplomats. In a letter home, the American ambassador to London, John Hay, summed up British and American frustrations with this new Canada. "Lord Salisbury, in a private conversation the other day, compared [Canada] to a coquettish girl with two suitors, playing one off against the other. I should think a closer analogy would be to call her a married flirt, ready to betray John Bull on any occasion, but holding him responsible for all her follies."

Yet the trade talks were successful and by Laurier's own estimation it would have been possible to put Canada's signature to "a very fair treaty," which would have opened the way to a continental free trade agreement (on better terms than the one the government of Brian Mulroney would

National Archives of Canada

The famous Last Chance Hotel (above) at Dawson Creek, around 1900. As the sign says, the establishment boasted what passed for "first class accommodations" and was open day and night. But the dogs had to stay outside.

Major Victor A.S. Williams, the commander of B Squadron, Canadian Mounted Rifles, astride his favourite horse, Joe. His little daughter, Phyllis, can be seen looking out of the door of the family's home near Winnipeg. Formed in the fall of 1899, the CMR left for South Africa in January 1900.

The answer was a typical Laurier compromise. There was no official Canadian military involvement, but Canadian volunteers were transported to South Africa at Canadian government expense, where they would serve under British command and be paid by Britain. The 2nd Battalion, Royal Canadian Regiment, made up of volunteers from across the country, was quickly brought up to strength (1,057 men and four nurses) and at the end of October 1899 they sailed from Quebec City to Cape Town aboard a converted cattle boat.

Startling Boer successes in the first months of the war suggested that what was really needed was not additional infantry (of which Britain had plenty), but mounted troops who could ride and shoot as well as the enemy. Ontario MP Sam Hughes argued that Canada had many such men, and the government listened. The Canadian Mounted Rifles were formed, mainly by recruiting adventurous young men serving in North-West Mounted Police detachments in the West. The new unit also recruited from among the ranchers and cowboys of southern Alberta.

Hughes wasn't alone in believing Britain needed Canadian roughriders in South Africa. Over Christmas 1899, Laurier received a telegram from railway millionaire Donald A. Smith, now Lord Strathcona and Canada's high commissioner in London. Smith offered to raise and equip a mounted regiment of 400 men, at his own cost. They, too, would be recruited from among the young men of the

Canadian North West: expert marksmen and riders who knew about roughing it in the wilderness. The first commanding officer of Lord Strathcona's Horse would be Canada's premier frontiersman, the NWMP's legendary Colonel Sam Steele, an Ontario-born veteran of the Fenian Raids, the North West Rebellion and the Klondike gold rush.

On January 21, 1900, the second contingent of Canadian volunteers, consisting of the two regiments of the Canadian Mounted Rifles and three batteries of field artillery (1,300 officers and men in all), together with 1,172 horses and a mass of equipment and ammunition, left Halifax aboard a convoy of three vessels. The 537 officers and men of the Strathconas would arrive in April 1900.

The Boers, meanwhile, were busy rewriting the manuals of warfare. Supplied by Germany with the latest artillery, machine guns and rifles (the deadly, rapid-fire Mauser), the army of farmers used hit-and-run guerrilla tactics to wound the British on the march, and long-range guns to harass British encampments and lay siege to major towns. The heavily outnumbered Boers became masters of surprise and deceit, often feigning surrender to draw Empire troops into ambush. When they could be brought to battle, they fought from carefully prepared defensive positions and trenches to wreak havoc on advancing lines of British troops.

The Royal Canadian Regiment (RCR) saw action at Paarderberg Drift in February 1900, as imperial troops under Lord Roberts forced the surrender of a force of some 4,000 Boers. Thirty-four Canadians were killed and 100 wounded in a courageous but unsuccessful assault on the Boer's hillside entrenchments, but the eight-day battle opened the way for relief of the besieged British garrison at Ladysmith - an event that was celebrated across Canada and throughout the Empire. The celebrations turned ugly in Montreal, where students from McGill University were incensed that French newspaper offices and buildings on the campus of the Université Laval were not flying the Union flag. There were violent clashes between French and English students and four days of rioting.

Despite the uproar at home, the RCR victory was one of the few British successes in what had been, up to then, a disastrous campaign. It was also the first overseas battle honour won by a Canadian regiment and is still celebrated each February by the RCR and its veterans.

Regardless of the Boers' early successes, the outcome of the war was never in doubt. By the winter of 1901-02 there were 300,000

Men of Lord Strathcona's Horse en route to Cape Town aboard the *S.S. Monterey* (above). The youngsters seated in front are the unit's buglers. A British general asked the Strathcona's commander, Col. Sam Steele, why he had recruited so many tall men as mounted troops? "These were the smallest I could find," replied Steele. The Manitoba Transvaal Contingent parading in front of Winnipeg City Hall (below) before leaving for Quebec City to join other troops from across the country. In October 1899, 1,039 men and their equipment were crammed aboard the *S.S. Sardinian*, an old cattle boat, for the 30-day trip to Cape Town.

Canadian troops camped outside Bloemfontein, South Africa. By the winter of 1901-02 there were 300,000 British and Empire troops in the country, and disease and hunger were rampant in camps such as this.

British and Empire troops in South Africa to confront a Boer army of about 70,000. The lopsided contest, however, brought its own peculiar problems. While it took an enormous effort for the British to keep such a large army in the field, Boer troops were able to regularly return to their homes to rest and recuperate - soldiers one day, civilians the next.

In an effort to deny the Boers this advantage, the British burned farms, destroyed crops and interned families in "concentration camps." There they were exposed to the same diseases which accounted for the majority of deaths among the British forces. With meagre rations and little medical help, 20,000 Boer civilians perished in what rapidly became a scandal in Britain. Public revulsion over the deaths of women and children was so serious it marred the final victory when the Boer army surrendered in May.

The Boers' tenacity had earned them grudging respect in Britain and the treaty ending the war was conciliatory. The Boers accepted British sovereignty while London promised protection for Boer language and religious rights and eventual self-government. Substantial compensation was promised for the farms which had been burned and the families who had been displaced.

The Canadians had made up a small part of the British force (almost twice as many Australians had served in the conflict), but they had acquitted themselves well. The original scepticism of British commanders, who thought the Canadians a ragged and undisciplined lot, gradually turned to appreciation for their courage and endurance. The Canadian infantry had taken part in some of the longest, most arduous marches in modern military history and

the mounted units had, indeed, been the equal of the Boer commandos. Four Canadians had been awarded the Victoria Cross. Of the 5,700 British dead, 135 were Canadian, although more had been victims of disease than Boer bullets.

On their way home the rambunctious troopers of the Canadian Mounted Rifles caused almost as much trouble for their fellow citizens as they had for the Boers. Discipline broke down on the long train journey west from Toronto. There was drinking and brawling, and the troopers' habit of shooting off their rifles terrified civilians along the route. When the regiment reached Winnipeg, police finally impounded their weapons. Trooper W.A. Griesbach, later to be mayor of Edmonton, recalled in his book on the war that his comrades were a decent lot, but their idea of a good time was to raise hell. "Men of this type require a rigid discipline and a good deal of casualties to reduce them to a proper state of mind. This we never had [on the trip home]."

The Strathconas, by contrast, enjoyed the hospitality and thanks of their namesake as they stopped in London on their way to Canada. Sergeant A.H.L. Richardson had been awarded the Victoria Cross for his bravery in rescuing a wounded corporal during a skirmish with the Boers on July 1, 1900, and Richardson and his compatriots were treated like heroes wherever they went. One British commander in South Africa, General Sir Redvers Buller, declared, "I have never served with a nobler, braver or more serviceable body of men."

It seemed, all things considered, a successful and mercifully short war and, above all, proof positive that when called upon Canadians could shoulder their responsibilities as the senior dominion. ■

Troops defending an area known as Honey Nest Kloof from Boer attack (above). This double-image, known as a stereo-gram, was one of a popular series of Boer War action photographs. With a 3-D viewer you could sit in your armchair and imagine yourself in the thick of the action. Members of the Royal Canadian Regiment cross a river near Paaderberg Drift (below) on Sunday, February 18, 1900. Later that day the Canadians charged a heavily fortified Boer position, with the loss of 21 dead and 63 wounded. Christened "Bloody Sunday" it was the costliest Canadian engagement since the War of 1812.

Sir Percy Girouard

The Canadian Who Built The Empire's Railways

Two great British leaders, Winston Churchill and Lord Kitchener, thought Percy Girouard to be one of the most brilliant and capable men of his time, but 70 years after his death few of his fellow Canadians would even recognize his name.

In an age of empire-builders the son of a Montreal lawyer and an American mother was among the most talented and ambitious. A graduate of the Royal Military College in Kingston, Ontario, in 1886 Girouard worked briefly as a surveyor with the Canadian Pacific Railway before joining the British Army and taking charge of the railway at the Royal Arsenal in London.

Railways were Girouard's passion and he was convinced of their potential in both war and peace. Few in the British military shared his beliefs, but in 1896 Kitchener was given the daunting task of moving an army and a vast array of supplies up the Nile into Sudan and he thought of the young Canadian who so relentlessly promoted rail power. Girouard was appointed the Egyptian Army's director of railways and given the responsibility of building track across the desert at the seemingly impossible rate of a mile a day. On their best day his newly formed railway battalion actually managed three miles and Girouard built a 600-mile track to supply Kitchener's army.

Sir Percy Girouard

During the Boer War Girouard's ability to build and manage railways once again enabled Britain to bring all its formidable military power to bear on the remote Transvaal and bring about a final victory. His reward was a knighthood and the opportunity to build a railway system to bind together the new Union of South Africa. Girouard went on to serve as Governor of Nigeria and then East Africa, building impressive railway systems wherever he went.

By 1914 Girouard's lessons in the importance of railways had been fully absorbed by the British Army and he was recalled, at the rank of major-general, to oversee the War Office Munitions Department and the transport of munitions to the western front. He died in 1932, a successful and wealthy businessman.

To many Canadians in the early years of the century, Girouard and others like him were living proof that they were part and parcel of a global empire of which they could be justly proud. Towards the end of his illustrious career, Girouard put it this way: "I stand as a British subject and a French-Canadian. My forefathers resided in Canada for 250 years. We have enjoyed under the British flag the Roman Catholic religion, the French language, the old Napoleonic and pre-Napoleonic law, without hindrance and with great tolerance." ■

Photos - National Archives of Canada

A field hospital at a Boer farmhouse near Paaderberg Drift, the day after "Bloody Sunday." The farmhouse and its stables were crammed with wounded, and a tarpaulin can be seen strung across the rear of the patio to protect casualties on stretchers from the fierce sun.

PART TWO

1900-1914

Sod-busting in Alberta, 1909, using one of the latest tractors. In the first decade of the 20th century dryland farming techniques imported from the U.S. West, and the increasing use of technology, revolutionized farming and brought millions of acres of new land under the plough.

Glenbow Archives

Canada West

THE LAST BEST WEST

HOMES FOR MILLIONS

RANCHING
DAIRYING
GRAIN RAISING
FRUIT RAISING
MIXED FARMING

ISSUED BY DIRECTION OF HON. FRANK OLIVER
MINISTER OF THE INTERIOR, OTTAWA, CANADA.

"Growing, Growing Growing"

Dreams Of Greatness In A Golden Decade

I think that we can claim that it is Canada that shall fill the 20th century.... For the next 75 years, nay the next 100 years, Canada shall be the star towards which all men who love progress and freedom shall come.

Sir Wilfrid Laurier

As the new century dawned, Victoria was queen, the 4th Earl of Minto was governor-general, 58-year-old Sir Wilfrid Laurier was prime minister - and Canada was riding a wave of enthusiasm, self-confidence and economic growth not seen before or since. Anything seemed possible. When Laurier famously declared that Canada would be the "star" of the 20th century, he wasn't simply mouthing empty, political rhetoric. He was expressing a point of view shared by many of his fellow citizens. They believed their country was on the verge of greatness.

It's hard for Canadians of the 21st century to grasp the boundless optimism of the first decade of the 20th. The world of 1900 seems remote and very different from the one we now inhabit. Popular prejudice encourages the view that late-Victorian Canadians were narrow, parochial and passionless; a stuffy, uptight generation. Yet while it is surely true that Canadians of a century ago, like all people, were limited by the conventions and prejudices of their day, it is also apparent they had vision, energy and confidence in such abundance that their great-grandchildren seem timid by comparison.

"We are a nation of six million people already; we expect soon to be 25, yes, 40 millions," Laurier confidently told a crowd in Toronto in 1904. "There are men in this audience who before they die, if they live to old age, will see this country with at least 60 millions of people." The popular prime minister was known for his hyperbole, not to mention his passionate nationalism, but he was far from alone in imagining such phenomenal growth. "Growing, growing, growing," wrote Stephen Leacock (better remembered by later generations for his humour, but in his time highly regarded as a social commentator). "A march that will make us 10 millions tomorrow, 20 millions in our children's time - and 100 millions ere the century runs out!"

"The Last Best West" (top left) was the most famous of the millions of Canadian government promotional fliers that flooded Britain, Europe and the U.S. at the end of the 19th century. The pitch to immigrants promised (in the words of one CPR advertisement) "the richest soil, the healthiest climate, and the cheapest farming land in the world."

Clifford Sifton (opposite page, inset) brought a knack for marketing and a messianic belief in western development to his role as Wilfrid Laurier's minister of the interior. Sifton's agents organized numerous travelling displays of Canadian agricultural productivity, including this overloaded bicycle and the "Girl From Canada" (left), which took part in all manner of parades and fairs around Britain to advertise the opportunities awaiting immigrants. The Canadian government emigration office (opposite page, top) at Charing Cross, London, was one of dozens of such offices throughout Europe and the United States.

Photos - National Archives of Canada

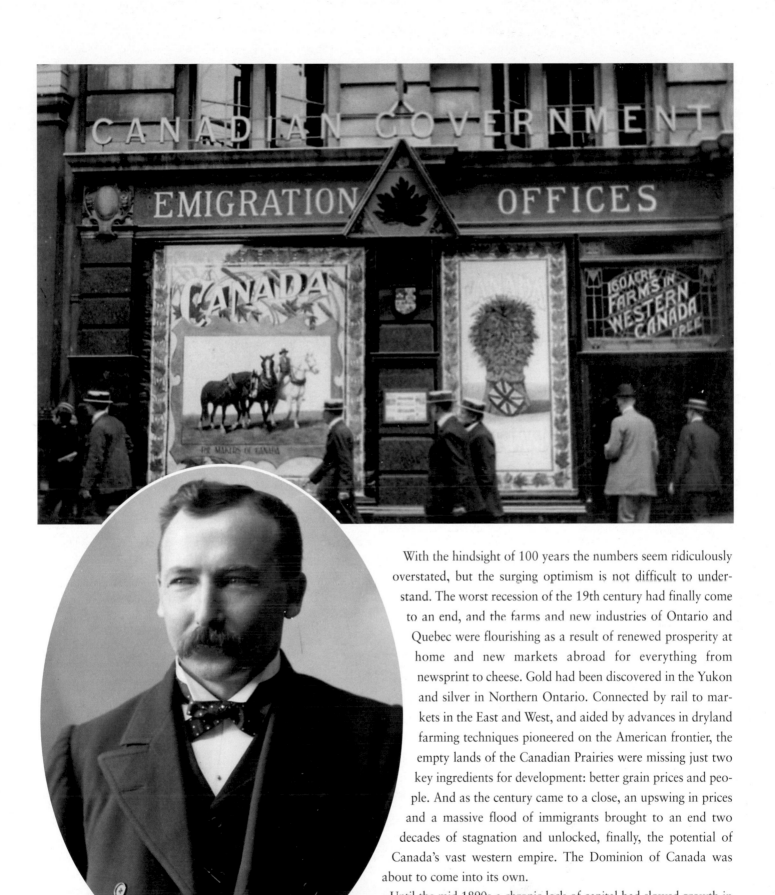

With the hindsight of 100 years the numbers seem ridiculously overstated, but the surging optimism is not difficult to understand. The worst recession of the 19th century had finally come to an end, and the farms and new industries of Ontario and Quebec were flourishing as a result of renewed prosperity at home and new markets abroad for everything from newsprint to cheese. Gold had been discovered in the Yukon and silver in Northern Ontario. Connected by rail to markets in the East and West, and aided by advances in dryland farming techniques pioneered on the American frontier, the empty lands of the Canadian Prairies were missing just two key ingredients for development: better grain prices and people. And as the century came to a close, an upswing in prices and a massive flood of immigrants brought to an end two decades of stagnation and unlocked, finally, the potential of Canada's vast western empire. The Dominion of Canada was about to come into its own.

Until the mid-1890s a chronic lack of capital had slowed growth in the world economy and demand for Canada's untapped resources. The Industrial Revolution appeared, literally, to be running out of steam and there was serious talk that the world might be approaching the limits of economic and scientific development. In 1893 wheat had reached its lowest price since the 14th century and recession in Europe and the U.S. had withered markets for Canadian exports.

The capital problem was solved by spectacular gold and diamond discoveries in South Africa, which pumped new fuel into the world economy. Markets recovered, began to grow, and there was money for development. The flow of investment capital into Canada quadrupled in the first two decades of the 20th century, totalling almost $5 billion - a staggering number for the times. The developing railway network and larger, faster ocean-going freighters brought down shipping costs. At the same time the frontier states of the American West seemed fully settled and people across the continent began to turn north, to "the last, best West" of Canada's Prairie and Pacific lands. It was a series of events tailor-made for rapid development, and the

result was an unprecedented, decade-long boom that made Canada the fastest-growing economy on earth and a magnet for immigrants who began to arrive in the hundreds of thousands.

Leading the immigration effort was Laurier's minister of the interior, Clifford Sifton. The Siftons had been among the thousands of Ontarians who had moved to Manitoba in the years after Confederation. Educated in Toronto, young Clifford became a lawyer and set up practice in Brandon, where he was elected to the Manitoba Legislature as a Liberal in 1888. After the 1896 federal election, Sifton was instrumental in helping Laurier negotiate a compromise allowing some French language education to continue in Manitoba. Shortly after, Laurier persuaded him to join his government and take on the critical task of populating the West.

Previous governments had been trying for decades to persuade people to move west, with varying degrees of success. The dynamic Sifton lifted these efforts to another level. With the aid of the shipping companies and railways he boosted promotion efforts and for the first time

Interior Minister Clifford Sifton's preference was for experienced farmers, but a cloth-capped army of immigrants (above), mostly male, arrived from the cities of Britain and the rest of Europe to work in Canada's rapidly expanding industrial sector.

A majority of immigrants to Canada early in the 20th century were single men, but there were also many families. Some, like this Scottish mother and her children (above), came to join men already established and hopefully able to provide for them.

looked beyond traditional sources of immigration. The Canadian West had, to that point, been populated mostly from Ontario and Britain. By the 1890s the only other significant immigrant groups were Icelanders on the shores of Lake Winnipeg and several thousand German Mennonites in southern Manitoba. All that changed as Sifton began to convince more European migrants to choose Canada over the U.S.

While Sifton's policies weren't entirely new (like his predecessors, he used the 1872 Dominion Lands Act, which offered new settlers 160 acres of land virtually free), he was far more aggressive in his approach to marketing. Sifton's belief in the West and its role in Canada's future was absolute and messianic. He lobbied Laurier for staff and money, and within a few years his ministry was distributing millions of pamphlets extolling the virtues of the Canadian West. These pamphlets - with titles such as "The Last Best West," and "The Wondrous West" - flooded Britain, Europe and the U.S., from Oklahoma to Moscow. They were accompanied by a small army of agents (mostly employees of shipping companies and the railways) who were paid $5 for every farmer they recruited, and another $2 for each family member. The prospective immigrants were promised, in the words of one CPR advertisement: "The richest soil, the healthiest climate, and the cheapest farming land in the world." As far as the richness of the soil and the cost of land were concerned, it was no exaggeration.

Until the outbreak of the Great War, more than a third of the immigrants to Canada would continue to come from Britain - and not all were received with open arms. Some were farmers or farm labourers (65,000 in the first half dozen years of the century), but the majority, members of Britain's army of urban, working poor, gravitated to Canada's growing towns and cities, where they competed for work with locals and often found themselves unwelcome. In the years prior to the war signs warning "No Englishman Need Apply" were not unknown. At the opposite end of the social spectrum, on the ranch lands of southern Alberta the "remittance men" - young scions of wealthy British families - were no more popular. They were often better known for their carousing and poor work ethic than for success as farmers or ranchers. The result was a widespread belief that the mother country was exporting its social problems to Canada.

Sifton certainly thought so. What he wanted, above all, were experienced farmers.

Until the Great War the majority of immigrants to Canada would continue to come from the British Isles. But British arrivals such as Mrs. Corbett and her family from Surrey, England (below), and this group of Scottish women (bottom left), were joined by increasing numbers of immigrants from across Europe - like this family from Holland (opposite page, far left), newly arrived at Quebec City in 1910. Courageous young Chadwick Sandles (opposite) travelled alone from England on his great adventure to a new home.

Photos - National Archives of Canada

"Agriculture is the foundation of all real and enduring progress," he argued. "We do not want artisans from the southern towns of England, who know absolutely nothing about farming." Nor did Canada need the "riotous, turbulent" overflow of Europe's teeming cities. The perfect immigrants, said Sifton, were stalwart peasants in sheepskin coats, "born on the soil, whose forefathers have been farmers for 10 generations, with a stout wife and half-a-dozen children." That was the way to populate Canada's empty lands.

And they came. Scandinavians, Austrians and Germans arrived in their thousands, and a small number of farmers were even recruited from France and Belgium. Yet the most significant group of new Canadians were "Galicians" and "Ruthenians" from the Slavic-speaking provinces of the Austro-Hungarian Empire. They were, in fact, mostly Ukrainian, and they would form the backbone of Sifton's army of pioneering farmers who would push the limits of prairie agriculture northward, clearing the bush as they went and bringing into production millions of acres of additional arable land.

Immigrants from Eastern Europe arrive at Toronto's Union Station in 1910. Writer Joseph Oleskow advised that it was important to leave behind the class-ridden attitudes of Europe. His advice to new Canadians was blunt and to the point. "Lift your head and look squarely into people's eyes... Don't bow and don't humiliate yourselves, because if you do free people will turn away from you in disgust."

National Archives of Canada

It is difficult to overstate (or perhaps even comprehend) the hardship and isolation experienced by these pioneering families in the first decades of the century. The climate was harder than many expected and not all the land was productive. As Sifton had foreseen, life was tough and in the early years the work was unending. Sometimes whole families would exchange rural hardship for better opportunities in the expanding towns and cities, and it was typical for younger men and women to find work off the farm to supplement family income.

Apart from the insistence that all children attend elementary school (and not even that in Quebec), there was no official government policy regarding the assimilation of the newcomers and no government services to help them adjust. It was generally assumed they would somehow be absorbed into the mainstream of Canadian life and conform to the values of society in general. And despite the desire of new Canadians to maintain their traditions and culture, there was indeed a widespread desire to embrace Canadian values and a new Canadian identity. In particular, education and proficiency in English were seen as the keys to a better life and involvement in the wider society.

Ukrainian writer Joseph Oleskow wrote in 1895 that it was important to leave behind the class-ridden attitudes of Europe. His advice was blunt and to the point. "Lift your head and look squarely into people's eyes instead of looking from under the brow like an animal chased by dogs. Don't bow and don't humiliate yourselves, because if you do free people will turn away from you in disgust."

Some were disgusted anyway. The *Nor'wester*, a Manitoba newspaper, expressed the traditional complaint against the immigrant: "Both economically and socially they will lower the standard of citizenship.... Not only are they useless economically and repulsive socially, but they will constitute a serious political danger."

Ambivalence towards the newcomers was common among those

Canadians who had been here for a generation or more. They were concerned that the growing wave of immigration would swamp the values, institutions and even the language of existing society. Stephen Leacock expressed a crude but typical view of the time when he wondered how a nation could be made out of "the dirtiness of the Doukhobors" or the "hungriness of the Hungarians." Manitoba Premier Rodmond Roblin fretted about the possibility of immigrants becoming a majority in western Canada and taking "all matter of government absolutely into their own hands."

Despite the prejudice, the opportunities for equality, freedom and a better life were real and most newcomers relished them. To say Canada's attempt to attract new citizens was successful is an understatement. The numbers are mind-boggling. In 1900 there were 5.3 million Canadians, but the first decade of the 20th century would see that population grow by 35 per cent to 7.2 million - and then jump another 22 per cent to 8.8 million by 1921.

About half of these migrants would settle on the Prairies, while another 40 per cent would gravitate to the expanding industrial centres of Ontario and Quebec. Only 9 per cent would go to British Columbia, and just

Two young immigrants to Lethbridge, Alberta (top left), from the Japanese island of Okinawa. In 1907 they were among the first group of Okinawans to emigrate to Canada. Identification of immigrants wasn't always so precise. This young immigrant to Alberta (right) is identified as "Ruthenian," but likely considered herself Ukrainian. No origin is recorded for these two children (bottom left), photographed outside Edmonton in 1910. They are posed with a stoneboat, used to haul away rocks from newly-broken land.

National Archives of Canada

An immigrant wagon train from the United States crosses a stream in southern Alberta. With $10 and proof of identity you could become the proud owner of a quarter-section of land. The settler then had three years to clear at least 30 acres for crops (or fence at least 80 acres for livestock), build a home and live in it for at least six months of the year. Do all of that, and you were awarded clear title to your own slice of Canada.

Glenbow Archives

PRAIRIE SCHOONERS.

"ALBERTA OR BUST" FROM UNCLE SAM TO CANADA

3 per cent would settle in the Maritimes. Between 1897 and 1911 more than 1.8 million immigrants arrived in the country, and for the first time most of them stayed rather than moving on to the U.S. On the Prairies almost a third of the newcomers were, in fact, pioneering Americans who had sold their farms at a healthy profit and moved north in search of cheap or free land. Their capital and experience in dryland farming techniques would have a profound impact on the successful development of the Canadian West. Not to mention its attitudes and politics.

By the early years of the new century Canada had become the world's leading exporter of wheat. The value of wheat and flour exports - $14 million in 1900 - would rise to $280 million and replace timber as the country's number one export and the foundation of the economy.

Two mowers cutting hay in Ontario. Traditional horsepower remained central to farming operations, but you could always call on a neighbour to help speed things up.

National Archives of Canada

In the years 1901-1903 the population of what would become the provinces of Saskatchewan and Alberta grew to 650,000, and as new farmland came under the plough wheat production soared to 100 million bushels a year. And still there remained a huge tract of Prairie land waiting to be settled and farmed!

Winnipeg was the hub of the prairie population and farming boom. Within living memory it had been a fur-trading outpost, accessible only by trail, river and portage, but by 1900 it had surpassed Halifax in population (42,000). It rapidly outgrew Ottawa (136,000 people) and boasted the largest railway yards in the world. Those rails connected the city and the West to the rest of the continent and the world beyond. Travel to Winnipeg from Toronto or Vancouver now took days rather than weeks or months, and the new rush of prosperity paid for electricity, telephones and streetcars - all the latest manifestations of civilization.

A boy ploughing the Barnardo Foundation Industrial Farm near Russell, Manitoba, around 1900. The foundation brought a total of 28,000 destitute or orphaned British children to Canada, and 800 boys were trained at Russell as farm hands. It was not always a happy experience.

National Archives of Canada

Like so many other Canadian towns and cities, Winnipeg had effectively made the trip from the 18th century to the 20th in a single decade - and that change was not always pretty or painless. One report described the city's north end as "a howling chaos, an endless expanse of mouldering ruin, a heap seething with unwashed children and sick men in grey underwear." An exaggeration, to be sure, but like all of Canada's bustling, booming cities, Winnipeg was showing the strain brought on by rapid growth, an influx of new immigrants and a chronic lack of housing and public amenities. Those things would come, but in the meantime the streetcars would have to coexist with mud and frontier chaos. It was a raucous mix, which would become typical of the burgeoning western towns and cities.

The large size of farms in the West, coupled with a shortage of labour, encouraged rapid mechanization. This early tractor was photographed ploughing William Hamilton's land near Hamiota, Manitoba around 1905.

National Archives of Canada

Charles Saunders

The Miracle Of Marquis

It is rare for a scientist to be credited with influencing the development of a country, and even more unusual when that scientist is a shy, poetry-loving musician whose original ambitions in life were to run a successful music school and master the flute.

Yet without Charles Saunders the settlement of the Canadian Prairies would not have been as successful and profitable as it was. Saunders made possible Canada's first and most spectacular economic boom by developing a tough, early-ripening wheat which produced the finest quality flour in the world and established the Prairies as a major exporter of grain.

Saunders was born in 1867, the same year as the country he would serve so well, in London, Ontario. He was one of five sons of William Saunders, the man who had persuaded Prime Minister Sir John A. Macdonald to fund research into crop varieties suited to the Canadian climate. All five boys worked with their father as they were growing up, and all were expected to join his crusade to revolutionize Canadian cereal production. But after studying chemistry at the University of Toronto and Johns Hopkins University in the U.S., Charles decided he was more interested in music. Together with his wife, an accomplished singer, he opened a music school in Toronto and wrote a magazine column about the city's developing music scene.

None of this impressed his father, who was still subsidizing his son's living expenses a decade later. In 1901 he finally lowered the boom and insisted Charles take a job at Ottawa's Central Experimental Farm (where Saunders Sr. was the director). His primary task was to create a hybrid wheat which could withstand the early frosts and pests that regularly wiped out farmers' crops on the northern Prairies.

It took four years of cross-breeding, using Red Fife (the dominant

National Archives of Canada

Dr. Charles E. Saunders in 1915. His development of a new hybrid wheat to withstand the Canadian climate made the Prairies the breadbasket of the world.

Canadian wheat) and hardy Asian varieties, before Saunders came up with an early maturing hard wheat which produced outstanding flour for bread-making. Over the next few years the new wheat, which Saunders named Marquis, was tested on farms in Manitoba and Saskatchewan. By 1912 the seed was generally available and by the end of the decade 90 per cent of the prairie wheat crop was Marquis.

Not only was the plant reliable and productive, it also quickly gained a reputation around the world for unparalleled quality. In 1900 Canadian exports of wheat and flour amounted to just $14 million. Within twenty years they reached $280 million-and seven decades later would top $15 billion! Saunders' hybrid was the foundation on which the development of the Canadian West rested-and with it the expanding prosperity of the entire country.

Saunders worked on developing other crop varieties until 1922, when failing health meant early retirement-and a welcome return to music and poetry. As his contribution to the development of the West became more widely appreciated he was awarded a state pension of $5,000 a year, and in 1925, at the urging of the Canadian government, Saunders was knighted. He died in Toronto in 1937.

In their 1997 book *The Canadian 100* (McArthur and Company, Toronto), which ranked the most influential Canadians of the 20th century, historians Jack Granatstein and H. Graham Rawlinson) rated Saunders-ahead of prime ministers Wilfrid Laurier, Pierre Trudeau and Brian Mulroney-as the individual having the most significant impact on the country. Deservedly so. His development of Marquis wheat made Canada the breadbasket of the world, brought in billions of dollars in export earnings and helped secure the prosperity of an entire country. ∎

Canada's agricultural productivity was so famous it became the subject of some well-intentioned humour in a popular series of cards published by the Canadian Postcard Company. Everything from three metre-high wheat (below) to giant pumpkins (above) was spoofed in the cards. It's not known if any of the distant recipients took them seriously.

"HER COURT WAS PURE; HER LIFE SERENE;
GOD GAVE HER PEACE; HER LAND REPOSED,
A THOUSAND CLAIMS TO REVERENCE CLOSED
IN HER AS MOTHER, WIFE AND QUEEN."

of Confederation - signalled the end of the Macdonald era. Tupper was replaced by another Nova Scotian, Robert Borden, but the Conservatives' rebuilding process would be slow.

As leader of the senior dominion, Wilfrid Laurier found himself at the centre of arguments over the political and economic future of the Empire. Joseph Chamberlain, the British Colonial Secretary, wanted an Imperial Council of colonial government leaders "to which questions of Imperial interest might be referred." It was clear this council would be an advisory body only - Britain would have the final say on all of the important issues - and Laurier wanted nothing to do with it. He toyed with the idea of colonial MPs sitting in the British Parliament (as was the case in France), but such a thing was never offered and Laurier eventually became a firm believer in Canada's full political independence under the British monarchy. He began a long, incremental process of increasing Canadian political autonomy that would not be complete until 1982.

On Tuesday January 22, 1901, the Empire lost its most enduring and unifying symbol. The bell at Toronto City Hall rang all afternoon, leading all other bells in the city in marking the passing of Queen Victoria. Thanks to the new Atlantic cable, the news was relayed from London only minutes after her death. As Toronto city council met in emergency session to plan public displays of mourning, businesses across the city closed and flags were lowered. Similar scenes

were repeated in communities across the country as people contemplated the end of the era which (even in the U.S.) had borne Victoria's name.

No monarch since, and few in the entire 1,000-year history of the British Crown, left such an indelible image. On the throne for 64 years, she was the only Queen most Canadians had known and her stern, no-nonsense matriarchal demeanour had come to define the age. All the more remarkable because, apart from great state occasions, the tiny, sombre queen had not been seen much in public for the greater part of her reign, preferring instead to perpetually mourn her beloved consort, Prince Albert. Yet during her rule Britain had become an undisputed superpower and the centre of a global Empire. Victorian Britain had become the wealthiest nation in history (even if that wealth was only a rumour to many of its citizens) and a world leader in science and the arts. God, the Victorians believed, must be an Englishman. How else could such a small island have become so great?

Canada, the first self-governing Dominion, was widely perceived as the elder child of the imperial family; proof positive that British culture and values could be successfully transplanted overseas. And at the heart of that culture and the values it espoused had been the dour

In the fall of 1901, the Duke and Duchess of York (the future George V and Queen Mary) arrived in Canada. This photo (below) shows the duke and duchess and their entourage on the steps of Government House, Toronto. The duke, on the far right wearing a bearskin, seems to be standing in a flower bed.

National Archives of Canada

The Duchess of York (walking between two unidentified women) at Poplar Point, Manitoba. For six weeks the royal couple toured the country in a specially modified CPR train. The royal visit enjoyed stunning weather and enormous crowds at every stop along the way.

National Archives of Canada

monarch who was not amused. She seemed to have ruled forever and her passing meant inevitable change. Not least for Canada, which was moving ever closer towards political maturity and greater independence, and which in the final years of Victoria's reign had begun to develop a character very different from that of the mother country.

Sir Wilfrid and Lady Zoe Laurier travelled to the coronation of 60-year-old Edward VII and Queen Alexandra, which was scheduled for June 26, 1902. However, Edward was taken seriously ill and the coronation was postponed to August 8. Not a propitious beginning for what everyone hoped would be another long reign. In the meantime Laurier attended a Colonial Conference timed to coincide with the coronation and he again stymied Chamberlain's attempts to tighten control over the colonies.

Laurier, as always, found the trip physically draining and on his return to Ottawa briefly considered resigning because of ill health. He was persuaded to stay on and in September the Duke and Duchess of York (the future George V and Queen Mary) arrived in Canada for a six-week

Like several other cities visited on the tour, Toronto built an enormous "Royal Arch" (below) to welcome the duke and duchess. As an experiment in public relations after the monarchy's long Victorian hibernation, the royal visit was a great success and would be the first of many such tours.

National Archives of Canada

tour of the country. They set off in a specially modified CPR train, and Laurier went with them - in his own private train. Laurier's political opponents complained that the trip cost $500,000, a fortune at the time, and that his rail car had been built in the U.S. rather than in Canada. Nevertheless, the royal tour enjoyed stunning weather and enormous crowds at every stop along the way. As an experiment in public relations, after the monarchy's Victorian hibernation, it was a stunning success. It would be the first of many such royal visits.

Laurier spent the rest of 1902 convalescing in the U.S. His colleagues covered for him by saying he was exhausted from fighting for Canada at the Colonial Conference. During his time in the U.S., Laurier was not entirely idle. He met with President Theodore Roosevelt and agreed on a process to resolve a lingering dispute over the boundary with Alaska. Canada had long argued

Toronto's bustling harbour, at the foot of Bay and York Streets. The young country was booming and self-confident, but the resolution of the Alaska boundary dispute in favour of the Americans was a blow to Prime Minister Wilfrid Laurier's drive for greater political independence.

for direct access to the Pacific to create an all-Canadian sea link between Vancouver and the Yukon, but the Americans controlled the coastline and for almost 70 years the U.S. ports of Dyea and Skagway had served the Yukon. A six-member tribunal of "impartial jurists" (three Americans, two Canadians, plus a British delegate to represent the imperial view) would meet to settle the issue, with a majority decision being binding on all parties.

Much to Laurier's chagrin, Roosevelt stacked the deck with three senators who had opposed Canada's claims. Still, with the support of the British representative Laurier was sure the situation would not be resolved on American terms. Or would it? It had been assumed that Lord Alverstone, the British Lord Chief Justice and London's representative, would vote with Canada, but Clifford Sifton - a member of the Canadian delegation at the talks - thought otherwise. In a letter to Laurier

he wrote: "I think the Chief Justice intends joining the Americans, deciding in such a way to defeat us on every point." The reason, suggested Sifton, was "a predetermination to avoid trouble with the United States" which under Roosevelt was aggressively expanding U.S. influence in the Caribbean, Latin America and the Pacific.

Laurier was outraged. "If we are thrown over by the Chief Justice, he will give the last blow to British diplomacy in Canada, "he warned Sifton. "He should be plainly told this by our commissioners." Alverstone was unmoved and voted with the Americans. At the signing of the new treaty in London in October 1903, the Canadian representatives refused to put pen to paper and walked out. Alverstone and the three Americans signed anyway, providing a majority and making the deal binding. The U.S. got everything it wanted and a gloating Roosevelt called it "the greatest diplomatic victory of our times."

Laurier, the anglophile and admirer of Empire, had been snookered. A chastened prime minister told the House of Commons: "I have often regretted that while the United States is a great and powerful nation, we are only a small colony, a growing colony, but still a colony. I have often regretted also that we have not in our hands the treaty-making power which would enable us to dispose of our own affairs." He conceded the obvious: "As long as Canada remains a dependency of the British Crown, the present powers which we have are not sufficient for the maintenance of our own rights." Britain had avoided an argument with the U.S. but had offended a great champion of British values and the Imperial connection.

Fire, Fire!

Canada's Booming Towns And Cities
Are Stalked By An Age-Old Terror

At the end of the 19th century, fire was the scourge of Canada's rapidly expanding cities and towns. Saint John, New Brunswick, in 1877; Vancouver and Calgary in 1886; St. John's, Newfoundland, in 1892; Dawson City, Yukon, in 1897 (and again in 1898 and 1900!); and New Westminster, B.C., in 1898 - all were ravaged by major fires.

Yet Canadians continued to be oddly fatalistic about fire. In the early years of the new century hardly any effort was made to prevent the ever-present menace. On April 26, 1900, the worst fire thus far in Canadian history destroyed two thirds of Hull, Quebec, within a matter of a few hours, killing three people and leaving 15,000 homeless. It was thought to have started in a chimney and spread rapidly through the mostly wooden buildings of the town. Sparks from the blaze ignited and destroyed several buildings on the Ottawa side of the river. The final tally of destruction was estimated at $100 million - a massive sum for the times.

The disaster prompted much criticism of the lack of modern firefighting equipment and proper planning to limit the spread of fire, but four years later in Toronto the lessons still had not been learned. Toronto in 1904 was typical of Canadian cities. Wood was

National Archives of Canada

The remains of the Currie Building in Toronto's commercial district, after the Great Fire of April 1904. The blaze that started in the building eventually razed 19 acres of the city's downtown.

Most fire-fighting equipment was still horse-drawn and rudimentary. In this dramatic photo (above) a team of horses from the Montreal fire department stands fast despite the smoke and flames. Busy wooden structures like Calgary's Sherman Roller Rink (below), used for all manner of activities from dance classes to concerts, were particularly susceptible to fire.

still the material of choice for most buildings, and even those built of stone or brick used wood for towers, dormers and decoration. There were few fire-resistant walls between adjoining buildings, and even fewer of the new sprinkler systems. To make matters worse, most commercial buildings now boasted electric lights - connected by poorly insulated wiring.

The night of April 19 was cold and windy when the fire hall on Lombard Street got a call to a fire in the Currie Building on Wellington West. By the time the horse-drawn fire wagons arrived the building was a mass of flame. It spread to other buildings close by and within an hour reached the *Evening Telegram* building on Bay Street, several blocks away, where a sprinkler system failed. Employees battled the blaze with buckets and hoses for two hours before fire crews could get close enough to help.

The 200-man Toronto fire brigade knew it was in danger of losing control and called for assistance. Firefighters from as far afield as London and Buffalo responded, but by the time what became known as the Great Toronto Fire was brought under control, just before 5 a.m., nearly 100 buildings and nineteen acres of the city's downtown worth an estimated $10 million had been destroyed. Several of the fire-gutted buildings smouldered for weeks, thousands of people were put out of work, but miraculously no one had been killed.

In the hot, dry summer of 1911, a fire swept through the area around South Porcupine, Ontario (above). The official death toll was put at 60, but it was no more than an educated guess and likely much too low. Below, the bodies of victims of the fire are evacuated from South Porcupine by boat.

It should have been a devastating blow to the Ontario capital, but the optimism and booming economy of the Golden Decade would not be denied. The cleanup and rebuilding began immediately, and within a couple of years hardly any evidence of the disaster remained. Indeed, most people thought many of the new buildings were a distinct improvement.

Downtown Victoria, B.C., suffered not one but two major fires in the first decade of the 20th century. The first, on July 23, 1907, began on the west side of the business district and quickly spread. The city's small but thriving red-light district was reduced to a smouldering ruin, as was a poor residential neighbourhood nearby, leaving 250 people homeless. Within four hours the fire had destroyed 100 buildings over five city blocks. Angry citizens complained that the fire department had neither the men nor the equipment to tackle a major fire and City Council vowed to make improvements.

It was just as well they did, since the devastated sections of the city had hardly been rebuilt when, just three years later, another major fire started in a department store and quickly spread to neighbouring buildings. This time the fire department was on the scene quickly and armed with new equipment, but the mostly wooden buildings burned so fiercely that they could barely control the blaze. It was eventually tamed with the help of troops from the city garrison, but not before it had done almost as much damage as the earlier conflagration. Yet, just like Toronto, the rebuilding was rapid and within a few years the twin catastrophes were all but forgotten.

Perhaps the most memorable fire of the era struck the Parliament buildings in Ottawa on February 3, 1916. The fire broke out in the Parliamentary Reading Room just before 9 p.m., sending MPs running for their lives as corridors quickly filled with smoke.

Then as now, winter fires in Canadian towns and cities were hellishly difficult to fight. This building (above), on Winnipeg's Bannatyne Avenue, is coated with a thick layer of ice after an overnight blaze.

The installation of electricity left many Victorian structures, including Ottawa's Parliament Buildings, vulnerable to electrical fires. After several smaller incidents, the original home of Canadian democracy was almost totally destroyed in February 1916 (above and left).

The blaze disrupted a debate on fish marketing regulations as terrified politicians scrambled to get out of the building. Prime Minister Robert Borden was forced to flee wearing a borrowed hat and coat.

The interiors of the majestic buildings were covered with wooden panelling, heavily coated with varnish. The wooden floors had been treated with oil and were also heavily varnished. Conditions were perfect for the rapid spread of the fire, and they were made worse by an icy wind sweeping across Parliament Hill. Within half an hour the roof of the House of Commons collapsed. The Senate Chamber lasted long enough for some senators and a group of soldiers to rescue paintings and other valuables before it, too, was engulfed in flames. When the blaze was finally brought under control around 3 a.m., the only building left intact was the Library of Parliament, which had been saved by its iron doors.

With Canada in the midst of war, rumours abounded that the fire was caused by German sabotage. An American newspaper had even printed a story alleging just such a potential conspiracy only three weeks before. However, a public inquiry found no evidence that the fire had been deliberately set. It blamed instead the lack of firebreaks and a sprinkler system in buildings that had suffered a dozen smaller fires since 1913.

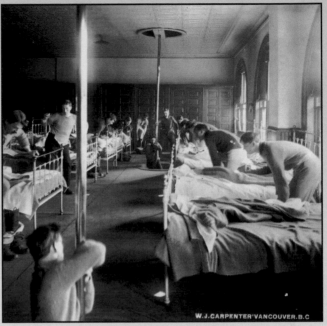

In response to the increased risk, towns and cities began to take a more professional approach to fire-fighting, establishing full-time fire departments and investing in new equipment. By the end of the first decade of the 20th century, Vancouver had modern firehalls (above) and even a motorized ladder truck (left).

A few months later fire struck again, this time in a collection of small mining towns around Matheson, near Timmins in northern Ontario. A hot, dry summer had left the forest along the Black River parched, and on the afternoon of July 29 the air was suddenly thick with smoke and the smell of burning wood. If Canada's expanding cities were poorly equipped to deal with fire, the small mining and lumber towns of the Canadian bush, and the pioneer farms which surrounded them, were utterly defenceless. Buildings were mostly wood and tarpaper, and firefighting equipment was rudimentary or non-existent.

Providentially, heavy rain slowed and then stopped the fire by the following afternoon, but in a little over 24 hours it had consumed 500,000 acres, leaving Matheson, Iroquois Falls, Kelso, Cochrane and Nushka in ruins. The fire had also done some damage in Timmins, but had been halted before it could spread.

The true horror of the Matheson fire was not revealed until authorities visited the farms and cabins in the bush surrounding the towns. Many people, including entire families, had tried to flee on foot but were overtaken by the blaze. Their charred bodies littered trails and roads throughout the area. The official death toll was put at 223, but it was no more than an educated guess and likely too low.

The rebuilding began immediately - using the same materials. As one survivor explained: "Money was in short supply, and wood was not." Besides, people had to be housed before winter arrived. "If the fire hadn't got you, a winter under canvas likely would." ∎

In the fall of 1904 Lord Minto was replaced as Canada's governor general by his brother-in-law, Earl Grey. The Mintos had been close friends of Wilfrid and Zoe Laurier and their encouragement of Laurier's policies had sometimes gone beyond what might be expected of an impartial representative of the Crown. Although Laurier was sad to see his friends depart, he welcomed Grey's appointment. The intelligent and outgoing Earl was a former politician with experience as an imperial representative (in Rhodesia). More importantly from Laurier's perspective, Grey was a Liberal.

Despite Clifford Sifton's insistence that Canada needed only farmers, not all the immigrants who arrived in these years went west to farm or populate the new towns springing up across the Prairies. Western settlement, a healthy export market and the rapid extension of the country's railway network had helped boost demand for all manner of industrial equipment and consumer goods. The resulting boom drew large numbers of immigrants to the manufacturing centres of southern Ontario and Quebec, which grew as quickly as or faster than the developing West. This explosive growth in urban population would have a profound impact on Canada's political and economic development through the 20th century.

In the twenty years from 1891 to 1911, Montreal grew from 216,000 people to over half a million. The largest city in the country, Montreal was Canada's industrial, transportation and financial hub. It was headquarters for the largest bank (the Bank of Montreal, naturally) and the biggest railroad (the Canadian Pacific), and home to most of the country's business leaders. The city's Dorchester and Sherbrooke Streets boasted mansions as large and grand as any to be found elsewhere in the Empire or in New York or Boston. An astonishing two thirds of the wealth of the booming country was controlled by Montrealers.

Montreal, Canada's largest city in the early years of the new century, boasted more impressive public and commercial buildings than anywhere else in the country. In this 1901 photograph of Place d'Armes Square (below) horse-drawn traffic still predominates, but so do utility poles and electrical wires.

The Bank of Montreal headquarters and Montreal's main post office in 1901 (below). The interiors of these grand buildings were no less impressive than their facades, as can be seen from this photograph of the main hall of the Bank of Montreal (right).

Photos - National archives of Canada

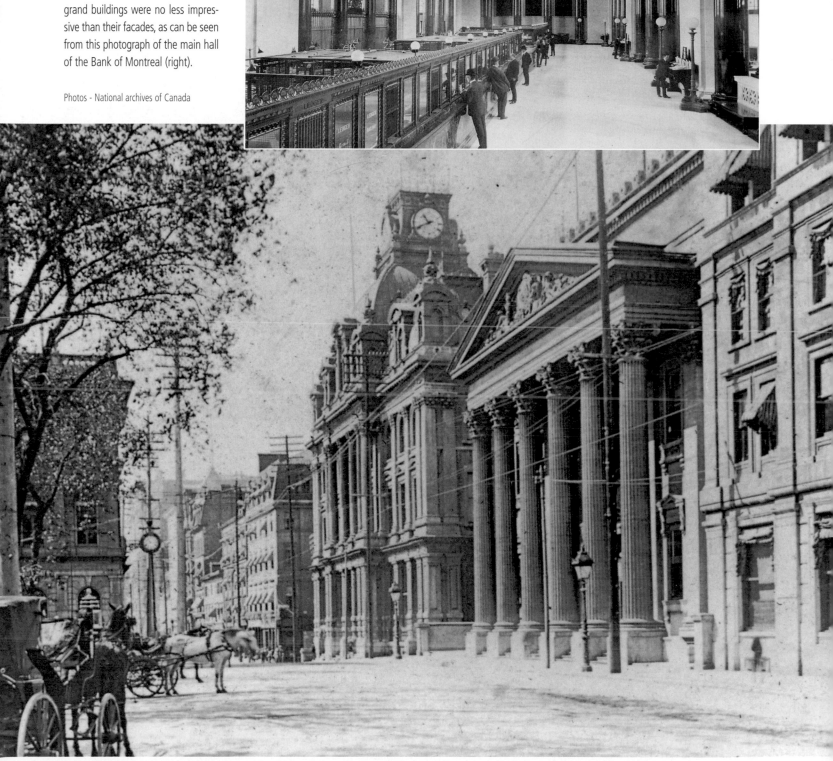

The growth of Toronto, which was then Canada's second largest city and rapidly becoming the centre of the country's manufacturing sector, was just as spectacular. Its population had exploded from 86,000 in 1880 to 208,000 by 1901. More than 90 per cent of its citizens were of English, Irish or Scottish descent, and over a third was foreign-born. Toronto benefited mightily from the construction of streetcar lines, which initially tracked the city's expansion to Rosedale and the other fashionable new suburbs being built north of Bloor Street, and later became the vanguard of urbanization, bringing more and more countryside within the scope of the city.

This boom had its darker side. Canada's cities had always had pockets of hardship, but now they harboured a substantial urban under-class. Montreal was afflicted with the highest infant mortality rate in North America (as high as Calcutta, India). In Toronto, too, at the end of the first decade of the 20th century, 55 of every thousand babies died before their first birthday. Canadian cities, wrote public health pioneer Dr. Helen McMurchy, were "still essentially uncivilized - neither properly paved nor drained, nor supplied with water fit to drink, nor equipped with any adequate public health organization."

The area around Halifax's main post office (below) served the Nova Scotia capital as a bustling public market. Such markets were very much a fixture in communities large and small. As in many other small towns, market day in Belleville, Ontario (bottom) brought in crowds from a wide area.

Photos - National Archives of Canada

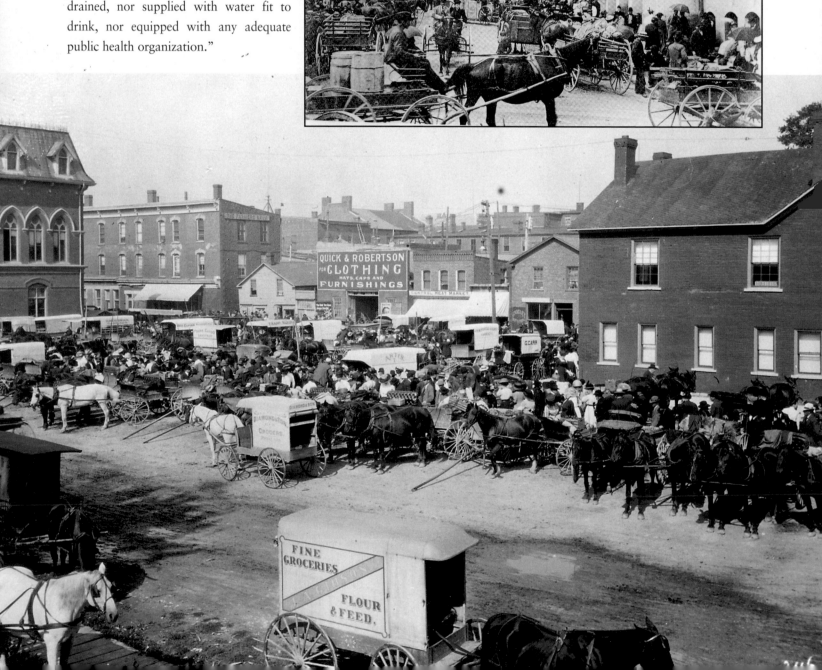

Sparks Street, Ottawa, in 1901 (above). Government transformed Canada's capital from a sleepy market town dependent on timber and agriculture, but the bustling Byward Market (right) - just a short distance from Parliament Hill - would continue into the 21st century as reminder of the city's agricultural roots.

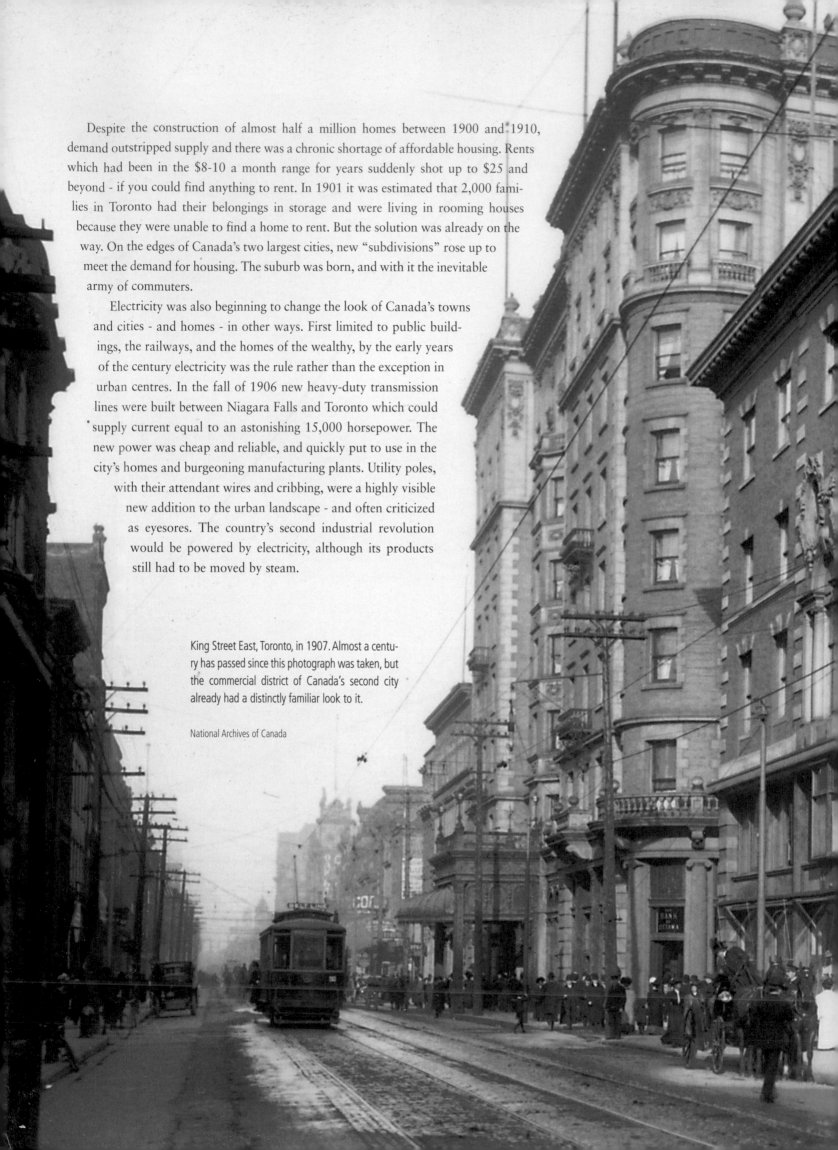

Despite the construction of almost half a million homes between 1900 and 1910, demand outstripped supply and there was a chronic shortage of affordable housing. Rents which had been in the $8-10 a month range for years suddenly shot up to $25 and beyond - if you could find anything to rent. In 1901 it was estimated that 2,000 families in Toronto had their belongings in storage and were living in rooming houses because they were unable to find a home to rent. But the solution was already on the way. On the edges of Canada's two largest cities, new "subdivisions" rose up to meet the demand for housing. The suburb was born, and with it the inevitable army of commuters.

Electricity was also beginning to change the look of Canada's towns and cities - and homes - in other ways. First limited to public buildings, the railways, and the homes of the wealthy, by the early years of the century electricity was the rule rather than the exception in urban centres. In the fall of 1906 new heavy-duty transmission lines were built between Niagara Falls and Toronto which could supply current equal to an astonishing 15,000 horsepower. The new power was cheap and reliable, and quickly put to use in the city's homes and burgeoning manufacturing plants. Utility poles, with their attendant wires and cribbing, were a highly visible new addition to the urban landscape - and often criticized as eyesores. The country's second industrial revolution would be powered by electricity, although its products still had to be moved by steam.

King Street East, Toronto, in 1907. Almost a century has passed since this photograph was taken, but the commercial district of Canada's second city already had a distinctly familiar look to it.

National Archives of Canada

As technological advances and demand for Canada's exports unlocked the country's economic potential, there were demands for an expanded rail system. Like Macdonald before him, Wilfrid Laurier was a firm believer in the nation-building potential of railroads. He launched a grandiose scheme to build a second transcontinental railway from Moncton, by way of the new mining towns of Quebec and northern Ontario, through Winnipeg and Edmonton to the Pacific at Prince Rupert. In 1904 Parliament approved plans for a government-backed project to build the first 1,800-mile leg from Moncton to Winnipeg. Known as the National Transcontinental, the project would (like many of the public-private rail partnerships of the 19th century) become mired in bankruptcies and mismanagement, but it would more than double the size of the national rail network, ease the flow of exports and aid in the development of a thriving manufacturing sector.

Although the direct involvement of government in the economy was still relatively minor, Ottawa was always being urged to do more in the name of nation-building. This was not a new idea. From the outset, the Atlantic provinces had been encouraged to view economic aid from the more prosperous provinces of central Canada as a major advantage of Confederation. Both the Conservatives and Liberals believed that the young country's economy had to be nurtured with public money and protectionist trade policies, which in practice meant subsidies for railroads and the fledgling steel industries in Nova Scotia and southern Ontario, and high tariffs on foreign imports.

Early on, Cape Breton became a showcase for economic intervention by Ottawa. Federal investment in the Dominion Iron and Steel Company plant at Sydney brought jobs and prosperity to the

The mud in this York, Ontario street may have been a playground to a small boy (above), but it was a major obstacle to the transport of goods around the Toronto area. Even in Canada's most prosperous province there were as yet few paved roads. But in the first dozen years of the new century the great movement from the country to the cities had begun. The growth was most spectacular in the country's half dozen largest communities, but the rapid urbanization also had a profound effect on market towns like London (opposite page, top) and Sudbury (opposite page, bottom).

Photos - City of Toronto Archives

island. Iron ore and workers were shipped in from Newfoundland and Nova Scotia's coal mining industry expanded to provide fuel for the steel mills. The industry transformed the economy of the area to such an extent that in 1906, for the first time in a generation, the Canadian Pacific abandoned its annual "harvest excursions" which took unemployed Maritimers to the Prairies to help bring in the harvests. For once, they could make a living at home.

The most aggressive public involvement in the economy came at the municipal level, where the pressure was greatest to provide the growing urban population with amenities and services. Until the late 19th century private monopolies were the favoured model for delivering power, water, transport and other basic services. But by the early 1900s Canadian public sentiment was warming to a different approach. If there was to be no competition, no marketplace, why not

In the early years of the 20th century, transportation and utilities were invariably provided by private enterprise, like this open street car (above) belonging to Ottawa's Electric Railway Company, photographed on Wellington Street in 1900. Public ownership was considered a radical idea, but not for much longer.

No city in Canada had changed as much as Winnipeg (below). Within living memory it had been a fur-trading outpost, accessible only by trail, river and portage, but by 1900 it had surpassed Halifax in population (42,000). The sumptuous Royal Alexandra Hotel (right) was the equal of anything to be found in Europe or the United States.

Photos - National Archives of Canada

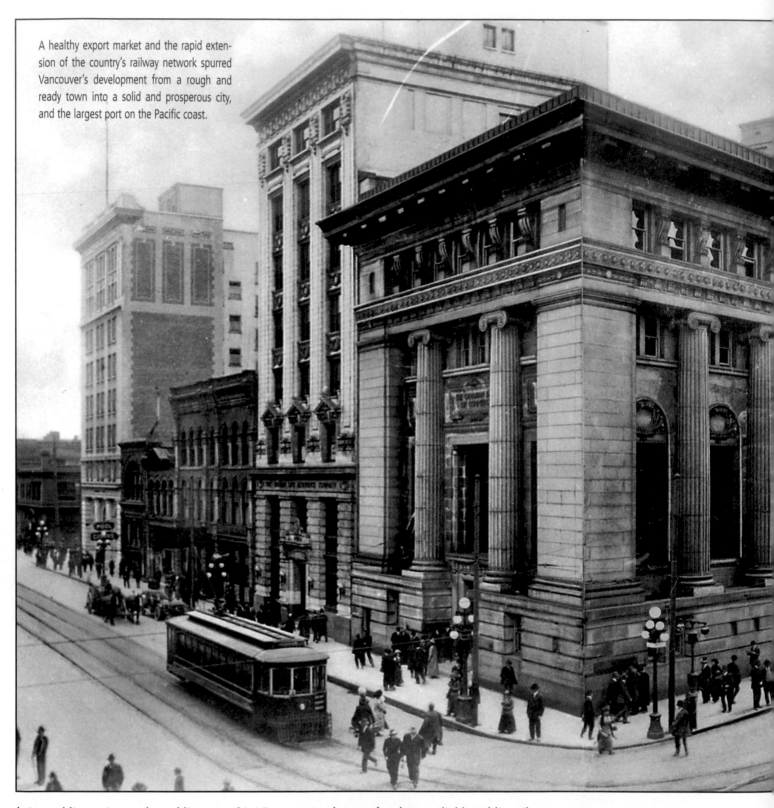

A healthy export market and the rapid extension of the country's railway network spurred Vancouver's development from a rough and ready town into a solid and prosperous city, and the largest port on the Pacific coast.

bring public services under public ownership? In a country hungry for cheap, reliable public utilities it seemed a persuasive argument and the result was a familiar blend of public and private enterprise, which would become a dominant characteristic of the Canadian economy for the next eight decades.

Perhaps the most remarkable (and most Canadian) instance of this new "public enterprise" took place in southern Ontario in 1906, where a coalition of businessmen, civic leaders, labour unions and clergy successfully argued that cheap electric power was best supplied by a government-run

monopoly. Led by Adam Beck, a cigar-box entrepreneur and provincial politician, they persuaded the Ontario government to create a public corporation to both generate and distribute electricity. Within a few years, the Hydro-Electric Power Commission of Ontario was being hailed as a model of efficiency and trusted steward of "the people's power." There were similar interventionist developments in the West, where first Manitoba and then Alberta and Saskatchewan took over the operations of Bell Telephone, claiming the company was too slow in extending telephone service to less profitable rural areas.

The shining star of Canada's private sector was Massey-Harris. By the turn of the century the Ontario-based farm implements manufacturer was the largest corporation in Canada and its products had an international reputation. In the first decade of the 20th century the company accounted for an incredible 15 per cent of all the manufactured goods exported from Canada. Its plants in Toronto, Brantford and Woodstock were marvels of mechanization. The company developed systems of mass production and standardized parts, which would be copied by an automobile industry looking to lower costs.

Massey-Harris was also one of the first companies in the world to create separate departments specializing in sales, advertising and accounting, and it pioneered the creation of dealerships where, in addition to buying equipment, customers could find parts and service. The company spent an enormous amount on research and development to keep one step ahead of its great American rival, International Harvester, and in 1910 it expanded production into New York State to tackle this competitor head-on.

The Massey family (like several other wealthy clans, including Toronto's Eatons and Montreal's Flavelles) were pillars of the church and leaders of a new mercantile elite. They practised generous philanthropy and made large contributions to the arts - including Toronto's first great concert hall - as well as a host of public charities. The Massey fortune, and those of other Toronto entrepreneurs, helped drive the social development of the city.

Massey-Harris was far from the country's only corporate success story. By 1910 a spate of start-ups and mergers had created a roster of company names which would be familiar to generations of Canadians, including the Steel Company of Canada, Sherwin-Williams Paints, Imperial Oil, Bell Canada and the Canadian Cement Company.

Canada's financial sector was also on the move. The Bank of Nova Scotia moved its head

office from Halifax to Toronto and the Royal Bank joined the Bank of Montreal in the country's largest city. As the banking business grew (from 300 branches in the 1880s to 4,500 in 1915), the number of banks actually decreased from 44 to 18 as some failed and others were absorbed into ever-larger institutions. Always careful and conservative, by the outbreak of the Great War Canada's banking industry had developed a reputation for stability and security rather than risk-taking, but it played a major role in financing the industrial development of the country. Although foreign capital would continue to be important in financing larger projects, the boom of the early years of the century created a pool of domestic capital almost twice as large as total foreign investment. Increasingly prosperous, Canadians had begun to invest in their own future.

Street urchins were a popular subject for photographers, but behind the images there was often a darker story. The photo of this shoeshine boy and his smoking pal (above) looks staged, but many young children were indeed called upon to supplement the family income. Fuel was expensive and collecting coal fallen from trains or delivery wagons (right) was as common as collecting bottles would be for later generations.

Canada's cities had always had pockets of hardship, but now they harboured a substantial urban underclass. Some of Montreal's poorer neighbourhoods (left) were as squalid as anything in Europe. The city suffered the highest infant mortality rate in North America (as high as Calcutta, India). In Winnipeg, an immigrant family rests on the sidewalk surrounded by meagre belongings (above). Work was plentiful, but getting established was a struggle for new arrivals. And Toronto's chronic housing shortage left many families homeless (right).

Edmonton's Jasper Avenue on Alberta's inauguration day, September 1, 1905. Over the next decade the city's population would rocket from 7,000 to 10 times that number. Calgarians could hardly credit that, with all their city's wealth and connections, it had been passed over as capital of the new province.

National Archives of Canada

In November 1904 Laurier led his party to their third consecutive majority. The election was a bitter personal defeat for new Tory leader Robert Borden, who lost in his own seat - along with the other eighteen Conservative members from Nova Scotia. The Liberal *Toronto Globe* whooped that "the government has swept the country in a wonderful way." There would, however be a silver lining of sorts for the Conservatives. Three months after the federal vote they would win a provincial election in Ontario, ending 32 years of Liberal rule. The result came as a

In the midst of the first great boom of the 20th century, times were often hard for the Native People who had so recently roamed freely across the Canadian Prairies. In this photograph from 1910, a Cree family supplements its income by harvesting sugar beet on a farm near Raymond, Alberta.

surprise to many, but it demonstrated a new inclination among canny voters to elect governments of differing political stripes to represent them federally and provincially.

The great project of Wilfrid Laurier's third administration was the reorganization of the Northwest Territories into the provinces of Saskatchewan and Alberta. The most contentious issues were the boundaries of the new provinces and, as always, minority education rights.

There were at least six serious proposals for splitting up western Canada. The one favoured

For many Canadians who grew up in the years before the Great War, it would be remembered as an idyllic time of freedom and peace. These girls (above) are taking part in "sports day" races in Toronto around 1908. Of course if you didn't disappear quickly enough after school you could always be called upon to tackle some household chores, like this trio hauling wood in Toronto's Bayview Park (left).

Photos - National Archives of Canada

The family of Hart Massey (above) at the dinner table in their Toronto home. The epitome of the stern Victorian, the founder of the agricultural implements empire (seated, far left) once placed his daughter Lillian on bread and water for having the temerity to wave to a boy from her bedroom window.

by NWT's Premier Frederick Haultain and a majority of the territorial legislature would have created one province encompassing most of the southern, fertile portions of present-day Alberta and Saskatchewan. Ottawa thought this new province would be too large, and Laurier worried privately that its political and economic clout could eventually rival that of Quebec and Ontario. The plan eventually adopted, creating two provinces split on a north-south line, was backed by powerful Edmonton Liberal MP Frank Oliver and Calgary lawyer R.B. Bennett, but supported by only seven members of the Legislature.

The NWT had reorganized education in 1901, establishing a "public" school system while allowing separate Catholic schools to continue. Catholic ratepayers could support their own schools and they continued to have their own inspectors, teachers and textbooks. Laurier liked the compromise, but he wanted constitutional protection for French education written into the legislation establishing the new provinces.

He was opposed by none other than Clifford Sifton, who was more concerned about the impact of the immigrants flooding into the West who were neither French nor English. He thought the best way to consolidate and Canadianize this new polyglot society was through a non-denominational public school system (i.e. Protestant) using one language of instruction - English. Sifton also considered provincial autonomy to be sacred. The BNA Act gave provinces the responsibility for education and Sifton didn't believe Ottawa should hamstring them with legislation which, in effect, told them how to run things. It was a classic federal-provincial division-of-powers argument, which would be repeated again and again throughout the century.

When Laurier wouldn't budge, Sifton resigned from the government and it seemed that others would follow. Faced with the possibility of a split in Liberal ranks, Laurier agreed to allow the new provinces to determine their own education policy. His decision upset his Quebec ministers and MPs, who had hoped to bolster the rapidly diminishing French presence in the West. Henri Bourassa, the leading Quebec nationalist within Laurier's caucus, saw the issue in dire terms: "I regret every time I go back to my province to find developing that feeling that Canada is not Canada for all Canadians. We are bound to come to the conclusion that Quebec is our only country because we have no liberty elsewhere." But Laurier insisted that practical politics dictated a compromise and convinced most of his MPs it was the only way to avoid the fall of the government.

The new provinces came into being on September 1, 1905. In Saskatchewan the economy was growing at a dizzying pace. The number of farms had increased from 13,000 to 50,000 in the first five years of the century, and wheat production would hit a whopping 26 million bushels in the harvest of 1905 - much of it destined for export. Agriculture was king in Alberta, too, and would remain so for decades to come, but a thriving coal mining industry already existed around Lethbridge and in the Crowsnest Pass and natural gas had been discovered at Medicine Hat and elsewhere. In 1905 there was a limited market for natural gas, but there were indications Alberta might also have oil - and that was already an important resource. There was even speculation that Alberta's energy and mineral resources might some day be more important than agriculture, but few people believed it.

First in Alberta (September) and then in Saskatchewan (December), the grateful citizens elected a majority of Liberals to form the first governments of the new provinces. There was criticism from opposition politicians that neither province had been given control over its potentially valuable natural resources, but it was not an issue which had grabbed the attention of most voters. Going down to defeat in Calgary was Alberta Conservative leader Richard B. Bennett, but it would not be the end of his political career. Canada would hear much more of Bennett, of oil and gas and of provincial control of natural resources.

At the same time as the new Prairie provinces filled with people and brought ever more land under the plough, the trend towards a more urban lifestyle was becoming universal across North America. In 1867 the vast majority of Canadians had been farmers, yet by 1905 one in three lived in rapidly expanding towns and cities and worked in the new manufacturing and service industries demanded by a growing country. In the first decade of the 20th century, Ontario and Quebec began the transition from rural to urban societies and were immediately confronted with problems

The increasing urbanization and industrialization of the early years of the 20th century had a major impact on Canada's larger cities, but elsewhere the pace of change was slower and life for most Canadians was blissfully unhurried. These boys are enjoying a summer afternoon diving off a pier in Sarnia, Ontario.

Photos - National Archives of Canada

Kicking up your heels was often frowned upon before the Great War, but that doesn't seem to be bothering these ladies (left) in Toronto in 1906. The good old hockey game, by contrast, was already a staple of Canadian entertainment. This game (below) is being played on an outdoor rink at Dawson City in the Yukon Territory.

of public health, education and housing. The problems provoked vigorous public debate and demands for change which governments found hard to ignore.

This was a time of social reform and expanding democracy, and it was becoming widely accepted that a healthy, educated population was the hallmark of a civilized society. The churches and civic-minded individuals still carried most of the responsibility for the welfare of society's less fortunate, but there was a growing confidence that science, education and proactive government could beat the age-old problems of poverty, ignorance and disease. Edwardians, like their Victorian parents and grandparents, knew that life was not necessarily fair, but unlike their forebears many were beginning to believe it should be. All it needed was individual effort, good government and, above all, Christian morality.

An Ontario family making maple sugar (below) in 1910. Not everyone made their own maple syrup, but before the advent of television making your own entertainment was definitely the name of the game.

National Archives of Canada

A baseball game in Riverdale, Toronto, in 1915. The first baseball game recorded in Canada was played in Beachville, Ontario, in 1838, and the London Tecumsehs were refused admission to the National League in 1877 because they refused to stop playing exhibition games against local teams.

City of Toronto Archives

Canada's growing urbanization had yet to have a profound impact on religion, which remained a great pillar of society. Clergy of all denominations worried about the pressures and distractions of urban life, but the disillusion and alienation which were already eating away at religious observance in Western Europe had not yet taken hold in Canada. It was an age of faith, and the majority of Canadians looked to their churches for moral leadership.

That morality was still essentially Victorian. In respectable, middle-class families, alcohol, dancing and music were frowned upon as threats to the moral fibre of the young in particular and society in general. Sunday was regarded as not simply a day of rest but of strenuous religious observance. For Protestants and Catholics alike, serious devotion meant that the entire day should be given over to attendance at church, contemplation of the Bible and the quiet enjoyment of family. No shopping or carousing.

Ontario's Muskoka Lakes region was prime summer cottage country for the prosperous new mercantile class, but even on holiday Edwardian formality was never very far away (below). At the end of the 19th century an electric railway had connected Preston, Ontario, with the outside world and turned the town into a thriving spa. It also prompted the building of several large hotels. This group (opposite page) is pictured in the grounds of the Hotel Del Monte.

National Archives of Canada

For those who couldn't afford an Edwardian summer cottage, or perhaps didn't want to dress for dinner, there was always camping and a few beers with your pals.

The involvement of the clergy in public life, if not always welcomed by politicians, was also an accepted fact. The influence of the Catholic Church in Quebec and the Protestant Orange movement in Ontario had been a central feature of Canadian politics for generations, but to this traditional involvement there was added a new "social gospel" advocating reform and collective responsibility.

The Protestant churches in particular became hotbeds of political activism. They agitated for industrial safety and public health legislation, and against child labour, prostitution and the demon rum. The ideals and clear goals of the social gospel gave the Protestant churches a new relevance in changing times and powered a religious revival. This was particularly the case

Taking a bracing stroll along the Lake Ontario waterfront (below) at Toronto's Canadian National Exhibition. Fresh air was also believed to be an effective treatment for tuberculosis. This young sufferer in Toronto (opposite, right) was given a cot and umbrella after he refused hospital treatment. He later died in the city's Weston Sanatorium.

Photos - City of Toronto Archives

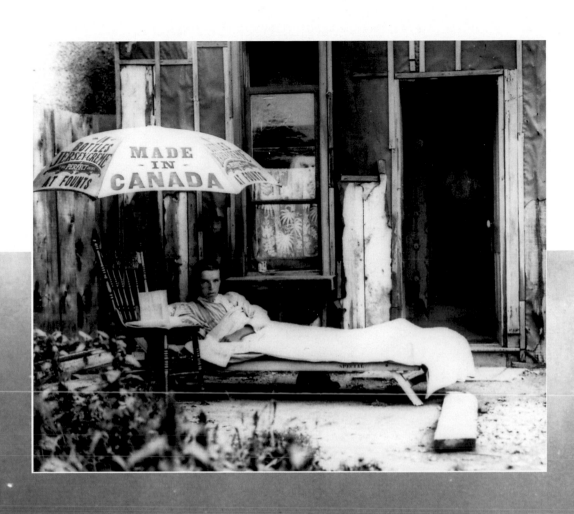

The E.D. Smith canning plant at Winona, Ontario (left), and fishermen unloading their catch at Prince Rupert, B.C. (above). In 1911 Prime Minister Sir Wilfrid Laurier thought central Canadian industry could weather a little competition for the sake of western development and campaigned in favour of "reciprocity" or freer trade with the U.S. A majority of the electorate thought otherwise.

Photos - National Archives of Canada

among the growing number of women who felt they had a special contribution to make in a crusade to uplift Canadian society. Indeed, Protestant reformism was at the heart of Canada's early women's movement.

In Quebec the reformist mood of the times had produced a similar doctrine of social Catholicism. Parish priests were often at the forefront of campaigns aimed at improving the quality of life of Quebeckers, but the church leadership resisted change in the name of religious orthodoxy. In particular it opposed any extension of rights for women, a concept viewed as an Anglo-Saxon Protestant perversion. Without the support of the province's dominant church, activists such as Marie Gerin-Lajoie concentrated on more practical issues (education and public health), and women's political rights took a back seat - where they would remain for another quarter century.

Despite the better economic times, Edwardian Canadians still married relatively late (the national average was 25 for men and 23 for women). Like their Victorian parents, most viewed the institution of marriage as an expensive and serious business, although almost 90 per cent eventually took the vows. Family remained the foundation of Canadian life, yet the Edwardian

generation produced far fewer children than the Victorians. Abortion and contraception were illegal (if not uncommon), but as prosperity and the involvement of women in the workforce spread, the birthrate declined by a staggering 40 per cent. Faced with a choice between large broods and material well-being, Canadians were simply opting for the latter.

At the same time they were healthier and living longer than ever before. A growing awareness of the importance of public and personal hygiene had a profound impact on the spread of the infectious diseases which had decimated earlier generations.

For the first time governments at all levels began to take on greater responsibility for the welfare and organization of society, most often by regulation but sometimes by direct involvement. In Ottawa the Board of Railway Commissioners was established to regulate the expanding rail system. The Quebec government made vaccination against smallpox compulsory, and in Ontario provincial

The crowded interior of a garment factory (above) in London, Ontario, 1910. It was noisy, dangerous work, but there was no shortage of labour. The Massey Harris plant in Toronto (right). In the first decade of the 20th century the company accounted for an incredible 15% of all the manufactured goods exported from Canada.

BE-52

National Archives of Canada

Steam drilling (above) at the Silver Lake Mine in eastern Ontario, 1908. A resurgent world economy created enormous demand for Canada's natural resources.

health inspector Dr. C.A. Hodgetts successfully championed similar legislation, pointing to the hundreds of unvaccinated people who were contracting the disease (153 in Sudbury alone in 1902).

In 1901 Ontario's new Bureau of Labour issued a scathing report on the prevalence of child labour. It charged that children as young as twelve were working long hours to help support their families. The bureau's secretary, Robert Glockling, acknowledged that some families would find themselves in dire straits financially if child labour laws were enforced or toughened, but he urged that critics keep in mind the greater good. "Individuals must be sacrificed for the sake of the general object of keeping children out of the mills and factories," countered Glockling. "If we make the exception we break down the whole law." And that was unthinkable.

Provincial governments were also gradually taking more and more responsibility for the regulation of education, although the quality of schooling continued to rely heavily on community support and the determination, professionalism and altruism of teachers. This was particularly true in rural areas, where teaching was often a solitary and isolated life. By the beginning of the 20th century most provinces had some form of compulsory education (Quebec did not), and schooling was generally available to "junior matriculation" level, or Grade 11. In Ontario, as a result of the demands of a growing urban middle class and the influence of its new universities, secondary education was increasingly available for five years or "senior matriculation." Still, secondary education remained the preserve of the most promising students and those who could afford the fees which were often charged. Pulling in the opposite direction was the ever-present economic pressure to get teenagers working. Before the Great War most jobs paid less than the $1,200 annual income considered necessary to support an average family of five, and the potential contribution of older children was important.

In October 1908 Wilfrid Laurier won an unprecedented fourth majority, a record which would stand throughout the 20th century. The Liberal leader had campaigned under the uninspiring slogan "Let Laurier finish his work," but the answer from the electorate was a resounding affirmative. Laurier revelled in his popularity, claiming that under his leadership "Canada has been lifted from the position of a humble colony to that of a nation." Despite a few discordant voices Canada was prosperous and united as never before. A policy of steady as she goes seemed eminently sensible.

National Archives of Canada

Waiting for dinner in the smoke-filled cook shanty of a logging camp in the Ottawa Valley (below). Despite all its obvious shortcomings, the cook shanty was the centre of camp life.

The famous "Diving Horse" at the Hanlan's Point fairground, Toronto Island, 1908. It was one of the more sensational, and popular, carnival acts of the era. The horse's opinion is not recorded.

City of Toronto Archives

A Nation Bound By Steel

Canada's Scandal-Plagued Second Railway Boom

"I n these days of wonderful developments," Wilfrid Laurier informed the House of Commons in 1903, "it is our duty, immediate and imperative, to build a second transcontinental railway." So began Canada's second great railway boom.

Much has been written about Ottawa's role in the development of the Canadian railway system, and there's no doubt it was marked by cronyism, scandal and enormous cost to the taxpayer. Railway building often seemed to bring out the best and worst in Canadians, and prompted Sir Edmund Hornby, the British railway engineer, to remark: "I do not think that there is much to be said for Canadians over Turks when contracts, places, and free tickets on railways or even cash is in question."

But it is also true that the building of the Intercolonial Railway (between Halifax and Quebec City) brought Nova Scotia and New Brunswick into Confederation, the Grand Trunk connected Canada with Chicago and the great markets of the U.S., and the Canadian Pacific made settlement of the West possible and linked distant British Columbia with the rest of the country. Without the 60,000 kilometres of track in place by 1915, Canada would not

In many ways this was the golden age of rail travel, and Canada's railways could offer much more than the crude "colonists' cars" that transported many thousands of settlers to the Prairies. Witness this comfortable Canadian Northern Pullman car of 1915 (above). A snowplough and its crew take a break in B.C.'s Selkirk Mountains (opposite, left). Then as now, keeping the route through the Rockies open during the winter was a constant battle with nature.

A small army of chefs, waiters, and porters ensured that the paying customers wanted for nothing while on board the elite transcontinental trains.

have enjoyed the economic and population boom that preceded the Great War. The development of the country ran on steel rails.

The second transcontinental route (the National Transcontinental in the East linking with the Canadian Northern in the West) made William Mackenzie and Donald Mann as successful and well known as the builders of the Canadian Pacific had been a generation earlier. And they benefited from a much better public image. "Service was our motto," explained Mann. "We had

more stopping places in 10 miles than any railway in the world." The railroad and the army of new settlers knew they relied upon one another. Trains would stop near isolated homesteads to drop off passengers and supplies, and in return farmers would keep an eye on the track and even make springtime repairs to the roadbed.

Access to the railway was vital to the growth of cities from Moncton to Vancouver as the ever-improving freight and passenger services effectively shrank the size of the vast country and

Snowploughs clear a path near the summit of B.C.'s Rogers' Pass. Before the automobile, this was B.C.'s only year-round, physical link with the rest of the country.

Part of the impressive system of bridges, tunnels and loops that carried the transcontinental line through B.C.'s Selkirk Mountains. It was engineering at its most extreme.

brought Canadians closer together. The railways made daily mail service possible between major centres, and by 1908 even rural communities had regular mail delivery. Improved transportation and communications made Canada manageable in a way it never had been before.

So despite the cost and the corruption, in the first decade of the century the architects of the rail system were lauded as few Canadian entrepreneurs have ever been. Mackenzie and Mann were hailed as nation-builders. Max Aitken, the future Lord Beaverbrook and a man not known for self-effacement, was one of many to acknowledge their achievement. "I was never a Mackenzie," lamented the founder of the Steel Company of Canada and British newspaper baron. "I created nothing as he did."

Still, in the end the critical importance of the railways to the national economy, the huge public investment and the continuing financial scandals plaguing the private companies which ran most of them, led to a series of nationalizations. By choice or by need, Canadian governments had long been in the railway business (par-

ticularly in the Maritimes) and by 1923 all of Canada's railways, other than the Canadian Pacific, would be brought under public ownership as Canadian National Railways. ∎

The other "last spike" photograph (top), taken April 7, 1914, at Fort Fraser, B.C. The last spike is driven home to complete Canadian Northern's transcontinental route. By this time rail travel was generally safe, but not without its hazards - as this train wreck at Azilda, Ontario (above) illustrates.

In 1910 Wilfrid Laurier made his first western trip in sixteen years, to see for himself the rapid development of the Prairies and British Columbia. He was warmly welcomed everywhere, making dozens of speeches; many late at night to crowds packed onto brand new railway station platforms in towns which hadn't existed a decade before. He spoke again and again about the "great adventure" which was Canada, and rarely missed an opportunity to encourage immigrants to vote: "The newcomer accepts the rights of this land and also the duties of Canadian citizenship, for where there are rights there are obligations." It had not yet become a political cliché and even the Tory press lauded him as Canada's "greatest son."

The trip was not without some controversy. Laurier was harangued on economic issues and on the unfulfilled goal of freer trade with the U.S. In Saskatoon he was accused of selling out the farmers who had supported him. One newspaper called it the "Arraignment of Sir Wilfrid." In Vancouver he was pressed on immigration issues and urged British Columbians to be open-minded and get along with the "Asiatics" who were their neighbours. The response was unenthusiastic.

Nevertheless, he returned to Ottawa full of typical Laurier passion for the emerging country. "I left home a Canadian to the core. I return 10 times more a Canadian. I have imbibed the air, spirit and enthusiasm of the West. I am a true westerner henceforth: nay, I should say a Canadian, for we must in future aim to know the West and the East only in emulation of the best in each other."

Behind the usual Laurier hyperbole was the realization that the peopling of the West had created another constituency to add to the country's volatile political mix. Laurier shrewdly realized that the western viewpoint, which did not easily accept the old bicultural definition of Canada, would

Sir Wilfrid Laurier (left), dapper as ever, on his last tour of western Canada in 1910. The trip included dozens of whistle-stop visits, including one to Mission, B. C. (right). Laurier returned to Ottawa and announced "I have imbibed the air, spirit and enthusiasm of the West." A year later he would be out of office.

National Archives of Canada

become more powerful over time and must be addressed if his Holy Grail of national unity was to be maintained. He was convinced that new economic policies were needed to reflect the country's rapid development, and he never doubted that his popularity and powers of persuasion could make them a reality.

But first he had to take a detour. In the early years of the century there was a naval arms race similar to the nuclear one six decades later. It was believed that Germany was building a navy to challenge Britain's century-old supremacy at sea, and with the Empire's far-flung territories this was a very real threat. Canada was prepared to do its bit and in January 1910 Laurier introduced a bill in Parliament to create a volunteer navy of five cruisers and six destroyers. Opponents poured scorn on the creation of what they called a "tin-pot navy."

National Archives of Canada

At the heart of the debate was the issue of independence within the Empire. The Conservatives supported more autonomy for Canada, but they thought Laurier was moving too far, too fast. Warships represented the ability to project power and in 1910 a navy was the ultimate demonstration of an independent foreign policy. Why, wondered the Tories, did the country need that? Laurier, as always, saw an opportunity to assert Canadian independence as part of the march towards greater political maturity. Canada was "the most anomalous [nation] that has yet existed," he told Parliament, and it was his task as prime minister to provide the symbols of national identity. "We are divided into provinces, we are divided into races, and out of these confused ele-

The 11,000-ton cruiser HMCS Niobe, Canada's first warship and the beginning of an independent navy. With 16 six-inch guns, 14 twelve-pounders, and three torpedo tubes, the warship looked impressive and was greeted in Halifax by cheering crowds.

ments the man at the head of affairs has to sail the ship onwards." If that ship were a Canadian warship, so much the better.

The government went ahead and bought the 11,000-ton cruiser *Niobe* from the British to serve as flagship of the new navy. With sixteen six-inch guns, fourteen twelve-pounders and three torpedo tubes, the warship looked impressive and was greeted in Halifax by cheering crowds. The *Niobe* was hardly cutting-edge technology, nothing like the new dreadnoughts being built by Britain and Germany, but it was still a formidable weapon for a Dominion wanting to flex its muscles on the world stage.

At the Imperial Conference of 1911 New Zealand (with prodding from Britain) proposed an Imperial Parliamentary Federation. Laurier opposed the idea, saying he could not agree to any plan which would make the Parliament of Canada subservient to any new political institution. He again opposed the creation of an imperial trade zone. What he wanted, and got, was an agreement that Britain would stop automatically binding Canada through imperial trade treaties. It was another step towards Laurier's goal of greater independence and on his return to Ottawa he made sure the point had not been missed: "I am happy to have seen at the Imperial Conference the triumph of the principle which ought to be the basis of the security of the Empire: it is that every community, society or nation shall govern itself according to the opinion of the people who comprise it."

An Unforgiving Ocean

Canadian Disasters Echo The Titanic

I n the late evening of April 14, 1912, 1200 kilometres from Halifax in an area of the North Atlantic notorious for springtime icebergs, the White Star liner *Titanic*, bound from England for New York, collided with a mountain of ice and sank early the following morning with the loss of 1,500 lives.

The most famous shipwreck in history is a cautionary tale which has fascinated people for nine decades. The owners' arrogant boast of invulnerability inspired the tragic confidence of passengers who clung to the myth and refused to fill even the limited capacity of the liner's lifeboats. Thanks to hugely successful books

and films, it is a story known to hundreds of millions of people.

Yet the sinking of the *Titanic* was but one of a series of disasters involving passenger vessels which would, over the next eight years, underline the sobering fact that, even in the age of steam and telegraph, the oceans off Canada's east and west coasts could be treacherous and deadly.

On May 28, 1914, the eight-year-old Canadian Pacific liner *Empress of Ireland* left Quebec City bound for Liverpool. Only two years after the *Titanic* disaster, no one claimed the ship was unsinkable, but she had been equipped with every modern safety

National Archives of Canada

The majestic Empress of Ireland. No one said she was unsinkable, but the ship had been equipped with every modern safety device.

The Princess Sophia (above) steaming through B.C.'s Inside Passage. The loss of the vessel in the dying hours of the Great War would generate lawsuits that dragged on for 15 years. No liability for the disaster was ever proven or accepted.

device - including watertight compartments designed to isolate damaged sections of hull. Perhaps most important to the sense of security felt by her 1,477 passengers and crew, and a direct result of the lessons of the *Titanic*, the *Empress* carried more than enough lifeboat capacity for everyone on board.

The night was fine and clear as 39-year-old Captain Henry Kendall took his ship out into the St. Lawrence River and headed towards the Atlantic. Kendall spotted the lights of another ship, the Norwegian freighter *Storstad*, about 6 miles off, making her way upriver to Montreal with a shipment of coal. As the two ships closed, a thick fog swept out from the shore and the vessels lost sight of one another for some minutes. Capt. Kendall maintained his course, brought the liner to a full stop and ordered two long blasts on the ship's horn.

For reasons never fully explained, when the fog rolled in the

Chief Officer of the *Storstad* had ordered a turn hard to port - towards the oncoming *Empress*. As the Norwegian ship cleared the fog it was no more than 100 feet from the liner and approaching at right angles. The collier's bow sheared through the side of the *Empress* and opened up a gash 15 metres high and 53 metres long.

The crew of the *Empress* (in the wake of the *Titanic*, well trained in emergency procedures and evacuation) rushed to close the watertight doors and launch the lifeboats - but the disaster unfolded too rapidly. In less than fifteen minutes the 14,000-ton ship was gone. Of the *Empress's* 40 lifeboats, only four had managed to get away. She sank so quickly that many of her passengers and crew were trapped below decks. Among those who managed to get into the water, many were drowned in a huge, spinning vortex as the engine-room exploded and the *Empress* went to the bottom.

As his ship went under, the explosion tossed Capt. Kendall

As dangerous as Canada's coastal and inland waters might be, the nation's trade relied heavily on merchant shipping of every description. In this photo, vessels line up at the docks in Port Arthur, Ontario (now Thunder Bay), to take on grain at the end of the 1909 shipping season on the Great Lakes.

from the bridge and miraculously he was spotted by a lifeboat. In the darkness, Kendall took command of the boat and began plucking others from the water. The *Storstad*, which had suffered superficial damage, also began picking up survivors. Soon two other ships arrived on the scene to complete the rescue operation.

It was Canada's worst maritime disaster. In all, 1,012 passengers and crew were lost, including 167 members of the Salvation Army who had been travelling to Britain for a conference. Out of 148 children on board, only four survived, and among 310 women passengers all but 40 lost their lives. The country was stunned. One Toronto newspaper called it "a loss too great to comprehend."

The west coast's worst maritime accident came four and a half years later, in October 1918, as another Canadian Pacific ship, the *Princess Sophia*, left Skagway, Alaska, in the midst of a blizzard

carrying 268 passengers; most of them Yukoners heading south for the winter.

Around 1 a.m. on October 23, as visibility deteriorated, the *Sophia* ran aground on the rocks of Vanderbilt Reef. The ship's master, Captain Louis Locke, wired CP's offices in Victoria to report that although he was stuck fast, the ship was not holed, wasn't taking on water and all passengers and crew were safe. He would not attempt an evacuation but would sit tight until the storm abated.

Throughout the following day, Capt. Locke and his crew were unable to free the *Sophia* from the rocks, but with other vessels standing by there seemed to be no immediate danger. Using a megaphone, Capt. Locke shouted to the American steamer *Cedar* that he felt there would be more risk in attempting to offload passengers in

In the early years of the 20th century shipbuilding remained an important Canadian industry, and not only the construction of ocean-going vessels. There was a thriving business supplying ships for the Great Lakes' trade, including the busy Collingwood Shipbuilding yard (pictured here) at Collingwood, Ontario.

high seas. He would wait until the storm subsided.

It was a fateful decision. Over the next 48 hours the weather stayed much the same while potential rescue craft hovered as little as 15 metres away. But on the afternoon of October 25 the storm suddenly worsened and the would-be rescuers were forced to seek shelter - leaving the *Sophia* pinned on the rocks as heavy seas pounded away at her weakened hull. At 5 p.m. the *Cedar* picked up a frantic wireless message: "We are foundering on the reef. For God's sake come and save us." The *Cedar* attempted to steam to the rescue but was forced back into the shelter of a cove. At around 5:30 p.m. she received another message from the *Sophia*: "Just in time to say goodbye. We are foundering."

The *Cedar* made it back to the reef at first light on October 26. It found a portion of the *Sophia's* bow but no survivors from among the 350 passengers and crew. For the next several days small boats worked to recover the dead. Amazingly, it appeared that two people had made it to shore (one to a beach some 25 kilometres from the wreck!), only to freeze to death during the night. One of the recovered bodies was carrying $120,000 in gold and cash, while another had a fortune in diamonds and rubies in a linen bag tied around the neck. Most of the bodies were shipped to Vancouver aboard CP's *Princess Alice*. She docked on the evening of November 11 as the city celebrated the end of the Great War.

A commission of inquiry found no one at fault for the loss of the *Sophia* and concluded that Capt. Locke's decision not to offload his passengers was "a matter of conjecture." Over the next fifteen years, lawsuits against Canadian Pacific would be pursued all the way to the U.S. Supreme Court (the ship had gone down in American waters), but no liability was found and no claims were ever paid. Yet shortly after the disaster CP quietly amended its standing orders, making it the first duty of a captain of a stranded vessel to get the passengers to safety. ∎

National Archives of Canada

Sir Wilfrid Laurier disliked automobiles, including his own (above). Under normal circumstances he preferred the tramcar, and on his way to work on Parliament Hill he would often enter into political discussions with other passengers.

Laurier called an election in September 1911, three years into the government's mandate, to decide the issue of "reciprocity" or freer trade with the U.S. Negotiation of the International Reciprocal Trade Agreement had been an unexpected coup for Laurier. The impetus for the deal came from the pro-free trade administration in Washington under Republican President William Howard Taft and provided for tariff-free entry for a wide range of Canada's natural resources and farm products, reduced rates for some manufactured goods and continued protection for other Canadian industries. In addition, whatever terms were given the U.S. would also be granted to the U.K. and most of the Empire. As an exporting nation, Canada had much to gain from a treaty which provided tariff-free (or at least tariff-reduced) access to such a huge market. It gave the West the export opportunities and access to cheaper American manufactured goods it had lobbied for during Laurier's western tour, while at the same time offering central Canada's manufacturing industries the compensation of improved access to U.S. and imperial customers. It was a classic Laurier compromise, and with everyone apparently a winner he foresaw no problem in selling it to the country. But for the first time his legendary ability to find the political centre on any issue had failed him.

Although Canada's manufacturing sector was now quite large - and in Laurier's view able to withstand competition - trade with the U.S. consisted mostly of the export of raw materials and the import of manufactured goods. That was particularly true of machinery and equipment. (Better than two thirds of the equipment and machinery which powered Canada's industrialization was imported from the U.S.) Canada was rapidly developing an almost symbiotic economic relationship with the U.S. which would eventually lead to the largest and most profitable trading relationship in history, but there was still considerable mistrust of American motives and concern over the ability of Canada's manufacturing industry to compete.

Joining Prime Minister Laurier on the hustings during the 1911 election campaign was a relative newcomer to Liberal politics, future prime minister William Lyon Mackenzie King (below). He is pictured here speaking at Simcoe, Ontario.

National Archives of Canada

With an overconfidence born of fifteen years in office, Laurier didn't think the trade pact could be seriously opposed. Even some Tories originally agreed, warning that the Liberal magician had once again come up with a winning issue. They were wrong. A coalition of manufacturers, railways, banks, and committed imperialists quickly came together and loudly denounced the treaty as treason, economic suicide, and the first step towards annexation by the U.S.

Some Liberals also opposed the deal, including the redoubtable Clifford Sifton, who concluded the cause of western development was for once trumped by the need to maintain the imperial connection. Even British author Rudyard Kipling, the very voice of imperialism, waded into the debate, declaring "It is her own soul that Canada risks today."

The Americans didn't do Laurier any favours, either. There were numerous comments from U.S. legislators suggesting (in the words of Congressman Charles Davis) that the goal was "to further amalgamate these two countries, and eventually make them one." Despite official denials from the Taft government, James Clark, the Speaker of the House of Representatives, vowed "we hope to see the day when the American flag will float over every square foot of the British North American possessions clear to the North Pole." His remarks were widely reported in Canada, and in some places widely believed. Earl Grey, the governor general, noted that "the feeling in Montreal and Toronto against the [trade] agreement could hardly be stronger if U.S. troops had already invaded our country."

Borden at last had a winning issue and the Tories campaigned under the emotional slogans "A vote for Borden is a vote for King and flag" and "A British subject I was born, a British subject I will die." In Quebec Henri Bourassa branded Laurier a traitor to his race, a sell-out to the British, and a promoter of Canadian involvement in the wars of Empire.

To Laurier, now almost 70, the strident rhetoric of his opponents was simply proof that his was the way of "moderation and conciliation" and the best course for the country. "I am branded in Quebec as a traitor to the French, and in Ontario as a traitor to the English.... In Quebec I am attacked as an Imperialist, and in Ontario as an anti-Imperialist. I am neither. I am a Canadian. Canada has been the inspiration of my life."

For once, Laurier's confidence in his own charismatic appeal was misplaced. He had been in power too long, and the country was neither as united nor as pragmatic as he had hoped. The voters returned 134 Conservative MPs to 87 Liberals, with the Grits losing 27 Quebec seats (40 per cent). "Lucky" Laurier had lost.

The biggest issue for Robert Borden's new Conservative government was the reworking of Canada's naval policy with a more pro-imperial emphasis. His solution was to provide $35 million to Britain for the construction of three new battleships for the Royal Navy, while keeping the country's fledgling navy (which by this time included a second light cruiser, the *Rainbow*). In 1913 a new Naval Aid Bill was approved by the House of Commons after a bitter and lengthy debate - only to be stalled by the Liberal majority in the Senate.

By the spring of 1914 there was still no clear policy on naval defence, but the issue was about to be overtaken by events in Europe. By mid-August Canada would be drawn into a maelstrom, which would test and ultimately confirm the young country's growing maturity. The cost on the battlefield was beyond the comprehension of most Canadians as they enjoyed the warmth of a spectacular summer, but it would be paid in full. ■

After 15 years in opposition, the Conservatives under Robert Borden (pictured here among a crowd of enthusiastic admirers) finally had a winning issue in opposing freer trade with the U.S. Laurier's legendary political instincts had finally let him down.

PART THREE

1914-1918

Men of the 16th Canadian Machine Gun Company take position in shell holes during the Battle of Passchendaele, 1917. In the mud of Flanders the Canadian volunteers would arguably become the most effective fighting force among the Allied armies, and through their suffering and success forge the beginnings of a national identity.

National Archives of Canada

A Young Nation Comes Of Age

Canada And The Great War

e entered the holocaust that was the Great War, if not exactly in the spirit of light opera, at least as if it were no more than the natural course of events.

John Diefenbaker

In Europe the signs of war had been building for a decade, yet the potential conflict seemed very far away and most Canadians were busy enjoying the glorious summer of 1914, blissfully unaware of the horrors to come. Barely a month before the outbreak of war, the *Toronto Globe* suggested that "relations between Britain and Germany are most satisfactory, and all their immediate interests are bound up with the maintenance of peace."

The light-hearted mood of the country seriously irritated visiting English poet Rupert Brooke: "What's really wrong with these damned Canadians is that at bottom they believe it's all play, and that war is impossible, and that there ain't no such place as the continent of Europe!" In letters home Brooke complained that Canadians were too darn busy enjoying their new-found prosperity.

In fact the economy had slowed from the hectic pace of the first dozen years of the new century. Inflated real estate prices, particularly in the new towns of the West, had pancaked, ruining many, but it seemed no more than a respite before the expected resumption of growth and the ongoing task of building the nation. Writer, temperance advocate, politician and suffragette Nellie McClung wistfully recalled that the arrival of war seemed to bring to a close "a very pleasant chapter" in Canadian life. She was right, although few if any Canadians had any idea of the impact this far off conflict would ultimately have on the country.

Most people assumed that if Britain were drawn into war, Canada would support the mother country. In fact, in response to the ominous signs in Europe the government in Ottawa had increased military spending to $14 million a year, bought new equipment, created new regiments and raised the strength of the militia to 75,000 men. Most received some rudimentary military

A trio of ladies in Edwardian bathing suits (left) enjoying the waters of Lake Winnipeg at Grand Beach, Manitoba. In the almost perfect summer of 1914, few Canadians were much concerned with the possibility of war in Europe.

National Archives of Canada

By 1914 the red-hot growth of the Canadian economy had slowed, but as these candid photos of Manitobans relaxing at Grand Beach illustrate, in the weeks before the outbreak of war in 1914 the public mood was generally relaxed and confident.

Photos - National Archives of Canada

National Archives of Canada

Younger Edwardian Canadians were often a good deal less formal than their parents, but it's clear from the attire of this group (above) that older Victorian notions of proper dress died hard.

training, but in truth the militia was more of a social club than a fighting force.

The young nation's most recent experience of war had been in South Africa at the turn of the century, and if a new conflict came it was expected to be a limited war along similar lines. Canada, as the senior Dominion, would do its bit but life would otherwise go on as normal. Few people considered the possible impact recent advances in science and industrial technology might have on the conduct of warfare.

In Europe in 1871 the union of German states under the Prussian royal house had created an aggressive new power. Germany's second emperor, Kaiser Wilhelm II (a grandson of Queen Victoria), believed his destiny was to make his country the most powerful nation on the continent. When Germany invaded Belgium and France on August 3rd, 1914, Britain stood by its treaty obligations and declared war. With scarcely any public debate, Canada enthusiastically followed suit. Belgium was a neutral country and the government of Sir Robert Borden argued that neutrality had to be defended and Germany's flagrant aggression stopped.

"Our recognition of this war as ours," said Borden, "determines absolutely, once and for all, that we have passed from the status of the protected colony to that of participating nation." At the time this was little more than political rhetoric, but the sacrifices of ordinary Canadians would make it reality.

Opposition Leader Sir Wilfrid Laurier backed Borden and called for Canadians to be of "one mind, one heart" in supporting the mother country in a battle to "save civilization from the unbridled lust of conquest and power." At the time most Canadians, English and French, agreed the cause was just, although they would come to disagree about the extent of Canada's involvement.

The announcement of war was greeted with scenes of jubilation across the country. In Montreal and Toronto there were huge demonstrations, the largest the country had ever seen, in support of Britain and the Dominion. The soldiers of the Empire would surely give the dastardly Hun a sharp lesson en route to a swift victory, and Canada had to play a part. An editorial in the Toronto *Telegram* praising the demonstrations summed up the mood: "It was the voice of Toronto carried away with patriotic enthusiasm at the thought that Britain, longing for peace, had determined to give the bully of Europe a trouncing!"

Kit inspection for the 11th Canadian Battalion at Valcartier, Quebec, September 1914. Morale was good, but few among the soldiers leaving for Europe had any understanding of the awful killing power of modern warfare.

National Archives of Canada

The convoy carrying the Canadian Expeditionary Force to Britain heading into the North Atlantic (above), October 1914. Most of the original contingent left from Quebec City, but by 1915 troop ships were leaving from ports across Atlantic Canada. This photograph (right) shows the Caledonia leaving St. John, New Brunswick, with the 26th Battalion and ammunition for the Canadian Corps.

Photos - National Archives of Canada

Copyright by
D. Smith Reid,
St John, N.B.

Robert Borden

The Reluctant Chief

In most Canadian histories the stern Nova Scotia Conservative who led Canada through the Great War takes a back seat to his more popular and charismatic Liberal opponent, Wilfrid Laurier. As a result, few Canadians know very much about Robert Borden or his considerable impact on the country.

A farmer's son, Borden was born in 1854 in Grande Pré, Nova Scotia. He was a successful Halifax lawyer before becoming an MP in 1896 - the year the Conservative dynasty succumbed to a rejuvenated Liberal party led by Laurier. Borden was a rather quiet and unambitious journeyman politician, which is perhaps why, in 1901, he was asked to accept the leadership of his fractious party. No one else seemed to want it.

In the House of Commons Borden was never able to match the style and panache of Laurier, but he was an effective speaker and Parliamentarian and for the next decade he managed to hold the Conservatives together as they waited for an opportunity to topple the seemingly unbeatable Liberals. That opportunity came in 1911 when Laurier campaigned in favour of a free trade pact with the United States. The idea was popular in the West, particularly among farmers who wanted cheaper manufactured goods and better access to the huge American market, but strongly opposed in the industrial cities of central Canada, which prospered as a result of protective tariffs and preferential trade agreements with Britain. Borden took up the cause of Canadian industry and successfully turned the election into a crusade in favour of traditional ties to the Empire and against any "truck or trade" with the Yankees.

As prime minister, Borden's pro-business policies were popular, for a while, but he put little effort into broadening his government's base of support and it became increasingly unpopular, particularly in Quebec. The Tories might not have been re-elected, but the outbreak of war in 1914 allowed the government to argue for a twelve-month extension of its mandate - by which time everyone

National Archives of Canada

Robert Borden swinging a golf club. The canny Nova Scotian proved to be a tough and determined war leader.

assumed Canada would once again be at peace. That didn't happen, and when the delayed election was finally held in December 1917, it took another overriding issue (conscription) and another appeal to patriotism to keep Borden at the head of a Union government made up of a coalition of Tories and pro-conscription Liberals.

Compared to the suave and popular Laurier, the careful and ponderous Borden invariably comes off second best. Yet the two shared some similarities. Both were hypochondriacs, constantly worried about their health and often contemplating resignation as a result. Like Laurier, Borden grew in office and sometimes surprised those who considered him indecisive (including Canada's disastrous wartime defence minister, Sam Hughes, who was stunned when the prime minister eventually demanded his resignation). And like Laurier, Borden grew into a passionate Canadian nationalist who believed in greater autonomy for the growing country.

He was often stubborn and unwilling to compromise and his lack of empathy for Quebec and the West, coupled with his stand on conscription (which he believed vital to winning the war), made him unpopular with many voters. But that same stubborn determination also made him an effective war leader. He supported Canada's commanders and soldiers in the field and regularly travelled to London to press the Dominion's view of the war. Canadian losses in the Battle of Passchendaele (16,000 dead and wounded) appalled him, particularly after British troops gave up the area a few months later without much of a fight. What had the Canadian losses been for? Shortly after, at a meeting of the Imperial War Cabinet, Borden is reputed to have seized British Prime Minister David Lloyd George by the lapels and declared, "Prime Minister, I want to tell you that if there is a repetition of the Battle of Passchendaele, not a Canadian soldier will leave the shores of Canada so long as the Canadian people entrust the government of their country to me."

As the terrible war came to an end, Borden was determined that the sacrifice of Canadians on the battlefields of northern France and Belgium and the enormous war effort at home must be recognized by Britain and the international community, and he was successful in placing Canada, for the first time, at the centre of world events. Ironically, in this he found an ally in Lloyd George, who had his own serious doubts about British conduct of the war and was a great admirer of General Arthur Currie and the Canadian Corps. Borden came to be viewed as an able and passionate defender of Canadian interests, and in many ways he was more respected in London, Paris and Washington than in Canada.

He also made good on early promises to promote social and political reform: the great causes of the day. His governments officially recognized trade union membership and the right to collective bargaining, enacted much needed civil service reforms and extended voting rights to women - all significant achievements for which Borden gets little credit.

He retired in 1920 (the first serving prime minister to do so) and died in Ottawa in 1937. His uncertain legacy was felt for many years. The divisions over conscription had deepened Quebeckers' mistrust of political leaders from outside their province - especially Conservatives - and they would effectively shut the Tories out until 1958. In the Second World War it would take five years for Ottawa to summon the courage to once more tackle the issue of conscription. And perhaps most significant of all, it would be three quarters of a century before another prime minister would campaign in favour of free trade with the U.S. ∎

A crowd in Toronto bids farewell to some of the first troops en route to the assembly point for the Canadian Expeditionary Force at Valcartier, Quebec.

Few Canadians in 1914 had any inkling of the slaughter to come. For the majority who were of British ancestry it was a case of the country assuming its clear responsibilities and an opportunity to show what Canadians were made of. But enthusiasm for the war was by no means limited to Canadians of British descent. Native Canadians, for example, enlisted in proportionately higher numbers than any other segment of the population. Despite the trials and upheavals of the previous century, almost a third of all Indian and Metis men of enlistment age joined up. It was, in the words of one soldier from southern Alberta's Blood reserve, a chance to show you were "as good as the next fellow."

Most French-Canadians were also horrified by Germany's actions and were sympathetic to the aims of the war - at least in theory. Even Henri Bourassa, Quebec's leading nationalist, was caught up by the mood: "Without a doubt, it is natural for any French Canadian to wish ardently for the triumph of Anglo-French arms." More than 50,000 French Canadians would eventually volunteer and many would make the ultimate sacrifice, but in general les Canadiens lacked the emotional attachment to Britain or, for that matter, to France, and there was widespread scepticism about involvement in an "Imperial" conflict which didn't directly threaten Canada.

English Canadians felt the French were shirking their duty in not volunteering in larger numbers, while French Canadians thought the Anglos' eagerness to fight betrayed a colonial mentality. But as long as service was voluntary, the division of opinion was nothing more than that, and an uneasy truce would prevail.

A review of Canadian troops at Camp Borden, Ontario (below). Fully 80% of the early recruits were British immigrants or Canadians of British ancestry, but that would change as the war in Europe ground on.

National Archives of Canada

Sam Hughes

A Loose Cannon Goes To War

The man who organized Canada's forces at the outbreak of the Great War, Sam Hughes, was as colourful as he was unpredictable. Canada's Minister of Militia and Defence styled himself "general," but it wasn't clear if he was entitled to the rank or if, in fact, he had any military experience.

Hughes was merely a Member of Parliament for the Ontario riding of Victoria North when he travelled to South Africa during the Boer War. Yet when he found himself in the middle of a Boer attack, he attempted to take charge of the Canadian line. Pistol in hand, he rallied the troops (who thought he really was an officer) with the cry, "Never mind me, boys, give them hell!" The British generals in charge certainly did mind and Hughes was packed off home, without the two Victoria Crosses he claimed he deserved.

What Hughes lacked in military credentials he more than made up for in bombast. Appointed Minister of Defence in 1911, he successfully badgered the Laurier government into accepting a $14-million military spending package: a large sum for the times. When war eventually came he ordered the flag above National Defence Headquarters in Ottawa flown at half-mast. Not to mourn the failure of peace efforts, but because Hughes thought the British had been too darn slow in declaring war!

As the man in charge of Canada's mobilization, Hughes was a disaster. Author Pierre Berton described him as "the wrong man in the wrong place at the wrong time." (*Marching As To War*, Random House, Toronto, 2001) Instead of following the official war plan, which called for Canadian forces to be assembled at an existing camp at Petawawa, Ontario, Hughes instead sent thousands of recruits to a barren piece of ground at Valcartier, Quebec, ostensibly because it was closer to the planned embarka-

National Archives of Canada

The unpredictable Sam Hughes.

tion point at Quebec City. (An old friend was subsequently given the contract to build a camp capable of accommodating 32,000 soldiers.) In October, as the main contingent of the Canadian Expeditionary Force was preparing to sail for Britain, Hughes insisted they take 6,000 additional men for whom there was no space - ensuring an overcrowded and miserable crossing of the North Atlantic.

Patronage was a Hughes' trademark, which he vigorously defended as cutting through red tape. He dispensed government contracts and created honorary colonels on a whim, with some very odd results. One of his strangest purchases was the MacAdam trench spade, which had a large hole in the middle through which soldiers could observe the enemy. Some 25,000 of the useless implements were eventually sold for scrap.

Stories of Hughes' blustering arrogance are legion. He once mistook a lieutenant for a captain, and when contradicted he promoted the startled officer on the spot. At the outbreak of war he created a Canadian Aviation Corps, with one plane and three officers, and shipped them to England with the first Canadian troops. The cabinet quietly killed off Hughes' unauthorized air force and the plane and airmen were left to languish in Britain.

Over the next two years, Hughes' inept management of the war effort led to a series of disasters, scandals and concerns over his mental stability. He was eventually replaced. Yet while Hughes is mostly remembered for his meddling and eccentricity, he was fiercely proud of his country and determined that Canada's contribution to the war effort should be both significant and properly recognized. That both goals were eventually met was due in some measure to the energy and determination of the pompous, bullheaded, thin-skinned Sam Hughes. ■

Native Canadian volunteers pose with a group of elders (left). Per capita, Canada's native communities supplied more recruits than any other group, often despite the grave misgivings of chiefs and elders. A winter under canvas in England took its toll, as witnessed by this funeral for a Canadian soldier (bottom left) in the spring of 1915. Once in France, the inadequately trained and equipped troops were given final instructions (below) before moving up into the front lines.

Photos - National Archives of Canada

Among the growing number of Canadians who were neither British nor French, attitudes towards the war were most often practical. If a son or sons could be spared from supporting the family or working on the farm, and if they wanted to be part of this adventure and prove their mettle, they could volunteer - and many eventually did.

But among the 1,100 men of the new Princess Patricia's Canadian Light Infantry regiment who left for Britain at the end of August 1914 (raised in only three weeks and paid for by Montreal millionaire Hamilton Gault), 90 per cent were British-born military veterans, and the rest mostly Canadian veterans of the Boer War. And of the 32,000 troops of the first contingent of the Canadian Expeditionary Force (CEF) who assembled at Valcartier and sailed from Quebec City in October, fully 80 per cent were British-born and a significant number were very recent immigrants. The slowing of the economy encouraged many to view service in the army as a temporary alternative to unemployment or occasional labouring jobs, and some undoubtedly saw it as a ticket home. After all, everyone agreed it was going to be a short war.

A few senior British officers and Canadian veterans had warned that the war might be long and hard, but politicians on both sides of the Atlantic had given the opposite impression to the public. There would be losses, in war there always were, but it would not take long to deliver

Artillery really came into its own in the Great War, with enormous numbers of ever-larger guns being produced. Barrages before an attack could involve thousands of guns firing millions of shells in an attempt to pulverize defences. The Canadian Corps became particularly adept at counter-battery fire (taking out enemy artillery positions).

National Archives of Canada

the Kaiser his comeuppance and the Empire's victorious soldiers would soon be marching home, covered in glory. With luck it would all be over by Christmas.

With the mobilization of troops came the first hints that what would become known as the Great War would be like no conflict which had gone before. The new railways and motor vehicles rapidly delivered hundreds of thousands and eventually millions of troops to the front - where the generals belatedly discovered that they lacked the necessary communications or tactics to effectively control such numbers. Equipped with the latest machine guns and the masses of artillery made available by modern industry, the largest armies ever assembled found that movement on the battlefield was difficult and attack murderously costly. The advantage lay in defence, so they dug themselves into the French and Belgian countryside in a system of trenches which eventually extended from the North Sea to the Swiss border.

In Eastern Europe, the Germans and their Austrian allies faced off against Russia. New

Canadian troops make their way forward through a shattered landscape (below). The technology available in 1914 allowed the rapid mobilization of vast numbers of men and machines, but communications were often overwhelmed by the size and scope of an industrialized battlefield.

National Archives of Canada

fronts would open up in the Balkans, the Eastern Mediterranean and in northern Italy, as Turkey and Bulgaria entered the war on the German side and Italy joined the Allies. There would be fighting in Africa and the Middle East. The Atlantic would become a deadly naval battleground where the distinction between warships and civilian vessels was quickly blurred. Troops from across Europe, Canada, India, Australia, New Zealand, South Africa and eventually the United States would become embroiled in the first global war.

On October 3, 1914, the main contingent of the CEF boarded a convoy of 30 ships and sailed for Europe. They were joined en route by a ship carrying the 500 men of the Newfoundland Regiment. Over the preceding centuries many European troops had made the journey westward across the Atlantic, but now for the first time an army of the New World was on its way to fight in the Old. The deployment of Canadian troops to Europe would set a precedent and a pattern for the new century, although none knew it at the time.

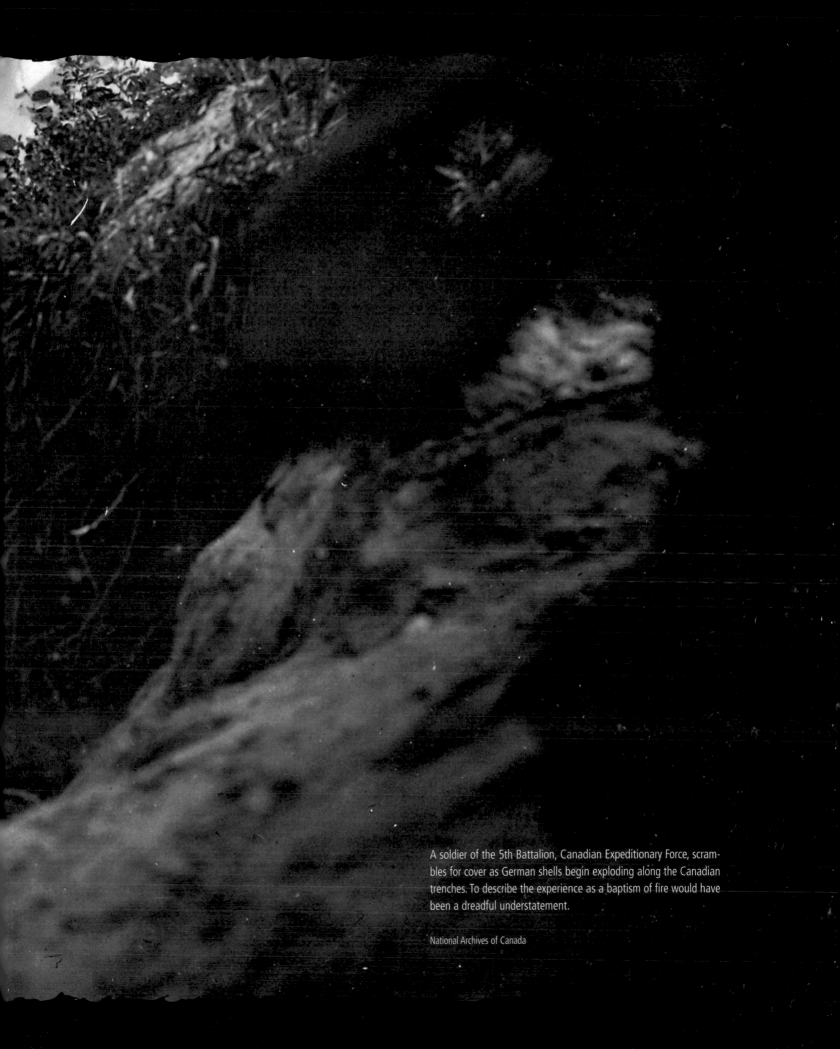

A soldier of the 5th Battalion, Canadian Expeditionary Force, scrambles for cover as German shells begin exploding along the Canadian trenches. To describe the experience as a baptism of fire would have been a dreadful understatement.

National Archives of Canada

John McCrae

Between The Crosses Row On Row

One of the few Canadians who thought the First World War would be anything but short and glorious was John McCrae, a 42-year-old doctor from Guelph, Ontario. He had served as an artillery officer in the Boer War and had witnessed what machine guns and modern artillery could do. "It will be a terrible war," he wrote to a friend.

At his age McCrae could have legitimately avoided service or worked in a hospital behind the lines. Instead he enlisted for combat. It was, he explained, simply a matter of duty. He was appointed brigade surgeon and second in command of the 1st Brigade, Canadian Field Artillery.

During the seventeen-day battle at Ypres in April 1915, Major McCrae tended the wounded at a dressing station dug into the bank of the Yser River and organized their evacuation down a muddy track. "All the tragedies of war move down that road," he wrote. "Wounded men limping or being carried; men crawling blindly; ambulances; shrieking horses; the cries of man and beast."

McCrae had no illusions about the war. In a letter discovered in 2001 by Canadian historian Michael Bliss, McCrae wrote to a friend that the fighting at Ypres had been terrible and "not the brief affair you might judge from the papers." In one 30-hour artillery duel with the Germans, McCrae's guns fired 3,600 rounds. Some of the guns "smoked at every joint" and were too hot to touch. "We lost very heavily (for artillery)," wrote McCrae. "But we have justified our existence. Of the 'horrors of war' we saw them an 'undred fold - at close quarters. From some of my uniform I can't get the bloodstains clear yet."

A few days after the battle had ended McCrae went behind the lines for the funeral service of a young officer he had known at McGill University in Montreal. The next day, sitting in the back of a field ambulance, he wrote the first draft of a short poem to the memory of his fallen comrades.

In Flanders fields the poppies blow
Between the crosses, row on row,
That mark our place; and in the sky
The larks, still bravely singing, fly
Scarce heard amid the guns below.

We are the Dead. Short days ago
We lived, felt dawn, saw sunset glow,
Loved and were loved, and now we lie
In Flanders fields.

Take up our quarrel with the foe:
To you from falling hands we throw
The torch; be yours to hold it high,
If ye break faith with us who die
We shall not sleep, though poppies grow
In Flanders fields.

On December 8, 1915, the poem was first published, anonymously, in *Punch* magazine. It rapidly became an elegy for a lost generation - and perhaps the most famous war poem of all time.

Later in the war, his health failing, McCrae was persuaded to accept a transfer to the Canadian hospital in Boulougne, where he became Chief of Medical Services. On the day he left the front there was another funeral. "We stood there while they laid away the sergeant who was killed earlier," he wrote. "I am sorry to leave them all in such a tight corner."

In January 1918, McCrae was appointed consulting physician to the First British Army. He appreciated the honour, but told colleagues he'd rather be with his beloved artillery. His fragile health had deteriorated rapidly and he died a few days later of pneumonia and a cerebral infection, never knowing that his words would live on as the quintessential soldiers' poem.

Harvey Cushing, an American doctor who had trained with McCrae at Johns Hopkins Hospital in Baltimore, was on hand when he died. "Never strong, he gave his all with the Canadian artillery during the prolonged second battle of Ypres," Cushing wrote in his diary. "Since those frightful days he has never been his old gay and companionable self, but has rather sought solitude. A soldier from top to toe - how he would have hated to die in bed."

McCrae was buried in the small war cemetery at Wimereux, France, on January 29, with an honour guard of soldiers, doctors and Canadian nursing sisters. They were followed by Bonfire, McCrae's horse, which had served with him since 1914. Appropriately, his colleagues from McGill managed to find a few winter poppies to lay on his grave. ■

John McCrae and his dog in 1914. The Guelph, Ontario, physician and Boer War veteran was one of the very few to comprehend the destructive power of modern weapons, and correctly predicted the war would be "terrible".

The first Canadian soldiers to reach France, at the end of 1914, were the veterans of the PPCLI and the Number 2 Hospital unit with 102 officers and men and 35 nursing sisters. The rest of the CEF - renamed the First Canadian Division - spent a miserable winter training on Salisbury Plain in western England (it rained for 89 of the 123 days the Canadians were camped there). The troops reached the Western Front on the Belgian-French border in the spring of 1915. Full of confidence and curiosity, these barely trained warriors, led by their equally green officers, were assigned a section of the line northeast of the

Wounded Canadian soldiers being evacuated on a light railway built to transport ammunition and supplies. During the Great War treatment of the wounded underwent a dramatic improvement, but it struggled to keep pace with the destructive power of machine guns and howitzers.

National Archives of Canada

Belgian city of Ypres. The harsh reality of the war was not long in coming.

On April 22, late in the afternoon, the Germans opened 6,000 cylinders and released 160 tons of chlorine gas on a slight breeze blowing toward the Allied lines. A green-yellow cloud, half a mile deep, blew over trenches to the left of the Canadians, held by the 48th Algerian Division and the French 87th. The Canadians watched as the deadly gas, hugging the ground, drifted through the French lines and occasionally blew into their own trenches. They had heard rumours of this terrible new weapon and realized what it was, but gas masks had yet to be issued to Allied troops.

Capt. F.A.C. Scrimger, a doctor with the 14th Montreal Battalion, passed the word that soldiers should urinate on their handkerchiefs or any piece of cloth and use it as an improvised gas mask. His unorthodox advice likely saved hundreds of lives.

The Algerians took the brunt of the gas and died or fled from their positions, many clambering into the Canadian trenches. As the gas dissipated three divisions of German troops wearing rudimentary respirators poured through what had become a three-mile gap in the Allied line. They occupied the French positions and rapidly began outflanking the Canadians. With pockets of gas still lingering on the ground, the troops closest to the French trenches (Toronto's 48th Highlanders and the Winnipeg Rifles) were ordered to counterattack.

The 'No Man's Land' in front of the Canadian trenches (below) after an attack near Courcelette, France. The area ahead of the front line was a murderous, muddy, killing ground churned by shells and swept by machine guns.

National Archives of Canada

A shell can be seen exploding a short distance away from an advanced dressing station (below) immediately behind the Canadian front line. Capt. Francis A. Scrimger, Medical Officer of the Canadian 14th Battalion, was awarded the Victoria Cross for his bravery in evacuating wounded men under heavy fire at a dressing station much like this one.

National Archives of Canada

Despite being seriously outnumbered they halted the surprised Germans. The fighting continued through the night and the following day, as the 1st Division repeatedly fixed bayonets and charged the enemy.

On April 24 the wind conditions allowed the Germans to again use poison gas. Once more the Canadians soaked handkerchiefs and rags in urine and tied them over their mouths and noses as crude protection. The effects of the gas were horrific. Men fell to the ground in convulsions as gas seared their lungs, but the Canadians held their ground against three successive German assaults. Albert Mountain Horse, a young lieutenant from Alberta's Blood reserve with Calgary's 10th Battalion, wrote home that the gas attack had been truly awful: "It was worse than anything

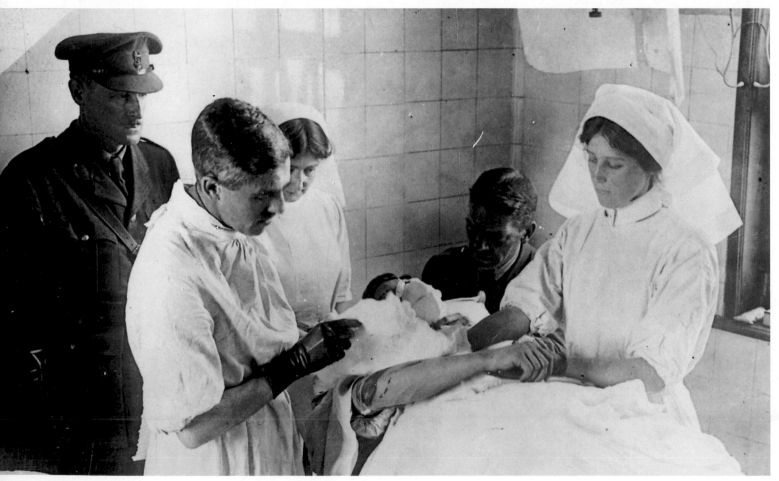

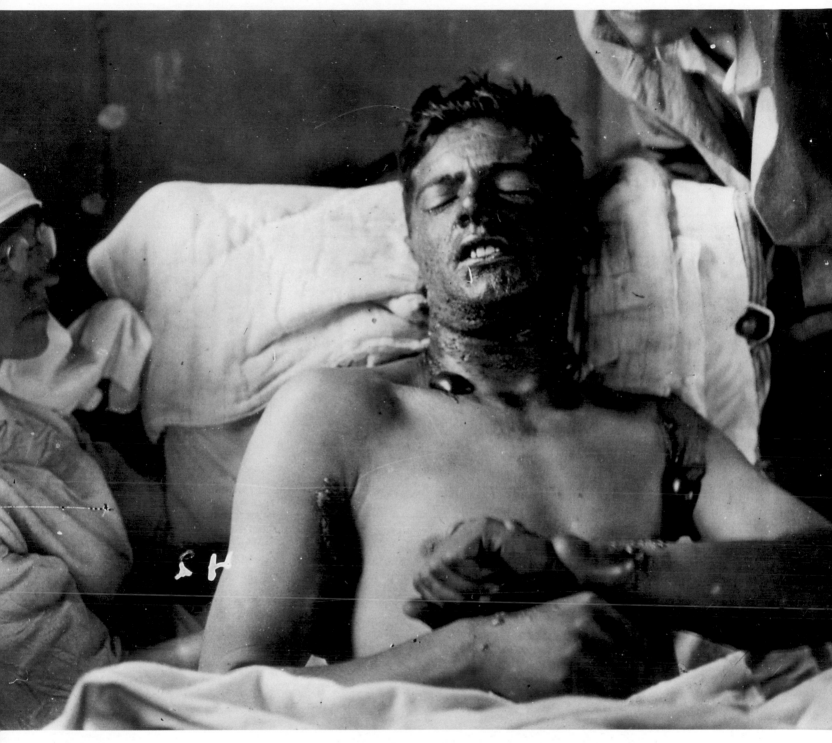

Photos - National Archives of Canada

An unidentified Canadian soldier (above) being treated for burns caused by mustard gas. Wounded troops in the admission area of the No. 2 Canadian General Hospital (top left) at Le Treport, France. And a soldier being operated on at a Canadian Field Ambulance unit (bottom left), allegedly within an hour of his being wounded.

I know of. I don't mind rifle fire and the shells bursting around us, but this gas is the limit." (Mountain Horse would experience three more gas attacks over the next few weeks and would die in November 1915 of an associated lung infection.)

By the time the two-week battle at Ypres ended, the inexperienced 1st Division had suffered 6,000 casualties, including 1,000 dead, many of them rookie officers. British commander-in-chief Gen. Sir John French wrote to the War Office in London: "The Canadians had many casualties, but their gallantry and determination undoubtedly saved the situation." It was the beginning of what would become a formidable reputation as front-line troops.

That first action at Ypres had, however, highlighted some serious shortcomings with

The Canadians developed a fearsome reputation among the German troops, but the Canucks were not without compassion. In the photo on the opposite page a Canadian speaks to a group of weary and shell-shocked enemy soldiers. Below, stretcher bearers and German prisoners evacuate the wounded.

Photos - National Archives of Canada

Canadian equipment. When the 1st Division went into action in Flanders, in addition to the gruesome reality of the battlefield, they discovered that their boots were next to useless and the Ross rifle, a fine hunting weapon based on the Austrian Manlicher rifle, was not rugged enough to withstand combat conditions. Both pieces of equipment came courtesy of political patronage directed to stalwart supporters of the Liberal government. The Ross rifle, a favourite of Militia Minister Sam Hughes and manufactured in Sir Wilfrid Laurier's Quebec constituency, was soon cursed by Canadian troops who found it needed constant cleaning and often jammed when the action got hot. Ironically, the rest of the British forces were equipped with the .303 Lee-Enfield, invented by Canadian James Lee, of Wallaceburg, Ontario. Reliable and tough, the rapid firing Lee-Enfield was so effective that German troops sometimes mistook it for machine-gun fire.

Politics followed the Canadian Corps to France. These troops (above) are voting in a B.C. provincial election.

National Archives of Canada

(Within eighteen months the Ross would be replaced by an improved Lee-Enfield rifle. Ottawa cancelled its contracts with Ross and in early 1917 the company went into bankruptcy, its buildings appropriated by the government. As late as 1940 the defence department would still have 75,000 Ross rifles in storage. They were sent to Britain at the outbreak of the Second World War to be used by the Home Guard, who were glad to get them.)

Despite their horrific introduction to combat, the Canadians had held their ground at Ypres and established a reputation for toughness and reliability. They were soon joined by three other divisions to form a Canadian Corps. The losses suffered during 1915 and early 1916 were staggering. The PPCLI was typical. After just ten months in Europe the regiment had suffered 921 dead and wounded out of the original 1,100 volunteers who had left Canada in such high spirits (267 killed, 60 missing presumed dead, 578 wounded and sixteen taken prisoner). Some of the wounded would return to the regiment, but it was clear that maintaining the strength of the Canadian contingent in Flanders would be a major and urgent challenge.

Winnie The Pooh

Harry Colebourn's Billion Dollar Bear

A chance, wartime meeting on a railway platform in northern Ontario led to the creation of one of the best loved characters in children's literature and a billion-dollar business. In August 1914 Lieutenant Harry Colebourn, a veterinary officer with the Fort Garry Horse, was travelling by train from Winnipeg to Valcartier, Quebec, to enrol in the Army Veterinary Corps. When his train stopped at White River, Ontario, he took a walk along the platform and, much to the surprise of his fellow travellers, returned with a female black bear cub. He had bought the orphaned animal for $20.

The cub accompanied Colebourn to Quebec, where it acquired the name Winnipeg and became the unofficial mascot of the 2nd Canadian Infantry Brigade. When the brigade shipped out to Europe the bear went with it and spent the next few months on the windswept Salisbury Plain in southwest England. In December, as the 2nd Brigade prepared to move to France, Colebourn wisely decided the battlefield was no place for a bear cub and persuaded the London Zoo to look after it - for a few weeks.

The animal remained at the zoo throughout the four years of war and by the time Colebourn (now a captain) returned to repatriate it, "Winnie" had become a favourite with staff and visitors, particularly children. Realising that the bear was content in her new home, Colebourn decided to leave her there.

One regular visitor was Christopher Robin Milne, son of author A.A. Milne, who was also serving in France. Winnie was the boy's favourite animal at the zoo - he named his own teddy bear after it - and to brighten up the grim war years the author began writing whimsical stories about Christopher Robin, Winnie (whom he changed into a male) and their adventures in a woodland area based on the Milne's country home in Sussex.

Photo courtesy The Fort Garry Horse.

Winnie with Harry Colebourn at the Canadian camp on Salisbury Plain, England.

Winnie the Pooh was published by Methuen in October 1926, and was quickly followed by two more books, all illustrated by E.H. Shepard. Winnie was an instant hit with old and young alike. The books have never been out of print and have been translated into almost every known language. The British editions alone have sold over twenty million copies (with sales in Canada and the U.S. easily doubling that number), but success wasn't finished with Colebourn's bear.

The *Winnie the Pooh* books had been favourites of Walt Disney's daughters, which inspired the world's favourite animator to bring Pooh to film in a 1966 cartoon. In 1977 Disney released *The Many Adventures of Winnie the Pooh*, the first feature-length animated film starring the little bear. Spurred by the astonishing success of the same when it was re-released almost 20 years later, Disney later made two more successful Pooh films.

According to the company, the films and subsequent video sales have made the bear the most popular animated character of all time - surpassing even Mickey Mouse. In 2000, total revenues from the Pooh empire (books, films, videos and merchandizing) amounted to more than US$1 billion.

At the end of the war Harry Colebourn, now a major, went home to Winnipeg, but he returned often to see his old friend at the London Zoo until she died in 1934. Colebourn continued to serve the needs of animals in the military and as a civilian veterinarian until his death in 1947.

In 1999 a party of officers and men from the Fort Garry Horse visited London Zoo and unveiled a bronze sculpture of Colebourn and Winnie. A copy of the statue also stands in the Winnipeg Zoo, honouring the world's most famous bear and a chance meeting which created a billion-dollar phenomenon. ∎

The Great War provided the first work experience outside the home for many Canadian women. In factories across the country, an army of women replaced the husbands, fathers and brothers who had enlisted. The munitions industry in particular could not have functioned without an influx of women. In the photograph at left an employee of the Fairbanks-Morse Company in Toronto makes six-inch howitzer shells. Bottom left, a woman at the Russell Motor Car factory, also in Toronto, works a lathe. Below on this page, shells on the assembly line at Montreal's Northern Electric Company.

Photos - National Archives of Canada

On the home front the reality of the war was slow to sink in. Censorship was tighter in Canada than in Britain and the country's newspapers reported every Allied attack as a brilliant success. The reality of the slaughter was mostly hidden from the public.

At the same time, anti-German propaganda cast suspicion on anyone of German ancestry (including the Royal Family, which changed its name from the House of Hanover to the House of Windsor). This anti-German hostility was no small issue in Canada, where immigrants of German descent formed the country's third largest ethnic group. German shops in Montreal, Vancouver and Victoria were attacked and there was enormous pressure on German-Canadians to declare their unequivocal loyalty, which many (but by no means all) were quick to do. The city of Berlin, Ontario, home to a large number of Canadians of German origin, changed its name to Kitchener as a patriotic gesture that paid homage to the British war minister, Lord Kitchener.

Immigrants who carried German or Austro-Hungarian passports and were of enlistment age were barred from travel to Europe. Nevertheless, some managed to cross the Atlantic to fight for the Fatherland, usually travelling via the U.S., which was still neutral. Throughout the war, when German and Canadian troops found themselves facing each other in the front line, there were repeated

instances of German soldiers calling out for news of Canadian cities and towns they had called home.

Early in the war, German-language newspapers in Canada were often outspoken in their support for the Kaiser's armies. They became more discreet as the war dragged on, responding to pressure from censors and several court actions brought by outraged members of the public, but it was the fall of 1918 before the government finally moved to restrict their publication.

Many immigrants from the Austro-Hungarian Empire, mostly Ukrainian, had roots less deep in Canadian society and were often viewed with greater suspicion than the more Canadianized Germans. All immigrants born in an enemy country were required to carry identification and register with the authorities, but of the 8,700 "enemy aliens" who were interned in work camps

Women soldering fuses at the British Munitions Company plant at Verdun, Quebec. By the third year of the war some 30,000 women were employed in plants such as this one, and Canada was supplying one-third of the munitions required by the Allied armies in Europe.

National Archives of Canada

across the country the majority were Ukrainian. The assumption of disloyalty was a bitter insult to these new Canadians, most of whom had little love for their former imperial masters. Some 10,000 Ukrainian Canadians eventually enlisted in the armed forces and Ukrainian churches were major contributors to the Red Cross and various funds to aid the war effort. It soon became clear to the government that most internees posed no threat. The majority were released and most camps closed - although 2,000 mostly German nationals would sit out the war in three camps in Nova Scotia, Ontario and B.C.

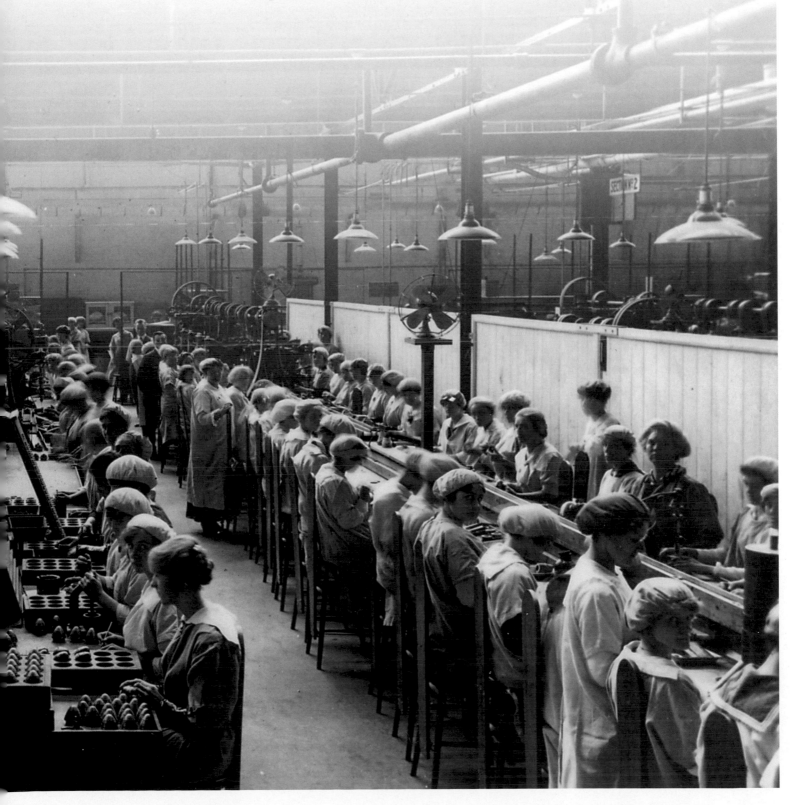

War production at the Canadian Linderman Company factory in Woodstock, Ontario. Canada's developing manufacturing industry received a major boost from the war effort, producing everything from uniforms, to munitions, and aircraft.

National Archives of Canada

German prisoners helping a wounded Canadian (left) near Arleux, France. And a Canadian sergeant (below) leads his weary platoon back from the trenches at the Battle of the Somme in November 1916. The Canadians had entered the front line in September, and by winter's end had suffered 26,000 casualties.

Photos - National Archives of Canada

These young officers didn't know it when they posed for this photograph, but among their number was a future Canadian prime minister. John Einarsson and Michael McMillan are pictured with a youthful John Diefenbaker (far right).

At the beginning of 1916, as Britain's losses mounted, Prime Minister Borden announced that Canada would provide a total of 500,000 men for the war effort. It was an astonishing number for a country with a population of around seven million, of which perhaps a million and a half were men between 18 and 35 who were fit to serve. Canada's defence budget would reach a staggering $331 million in 1916 (a 23-fold increase from 1914). Unemployment disappeared almost overnight as the recruitment drive went into high gear and those not in uniform were absorbed by Canada's factories and farms, now straining to produce munitions and food for the war effort.

The question was, would it be enough?

The weaponry and manpower made available by industrial society far outstripped military doctrine still rooted in the 19th century. Senior German and Allied generals were convinced that a victory on the battlefield was vital if the war was to be brought to a decisive end. Again and again, massive infantry assaults, backed by overwhelming artillery support, were launched in vain attempts to achieve the elusive "breakthrough." The result was slaughter on a mind-numbing scale. On July 1, 1916, along the Somme River in northern France, British forces launched just such an attack. On the first day of the battle British forces suffered 60,000 casualties (20,000 dead), and some units - the Newfoundland Regiment among them - were obliterated. By the time the Somme fighting ended in November the cost would be counted in numbers beyond comprehension: 624,000 Allied dead and wounded, 660,000 German. All for an advance of less than 13 kilometres and control of a sliver of territory of little strategic importance.

Throughout that long year the Canadians distinguished themselves at St-Eloi, Courcelette and on the Somme. Britain's new prime minister, David Lloyd George, was so impressed he insisted the Canadians and the Australians be regarded as the "shock troops" of the Allied forces.

The search for any battlefield advantage led to larger and larger pieces of artillery. These converted naval guns are being used by the Canadian artillery to shell German positions in the "softening up" process before the attack on Vimy Ridge.

Two Canadians (right) examine a grim reminder that their battle for Vimy Ridge was not the first. In two unsuccessful attacks on the ridge in 1915, the French army had suffered 300,000 dead and wounded.

But the cost had been high. The number of dead was approaching 35,000 and the arrival of fresh troops from Canada was falling dramatically short of replacing the casualties. Between the summer of 1916 and the fall of 1917, less than 3,000 recruits joined the Canadian forces in Europe. The naiveté of 1914 had worn off and censorship could no longer hide the losses.

1917 would be a year of trial and triumph for the Canadians. It began with the Corps preparing for an assault against heavily fortified German positions on a steep escarpment near the French city of Arras. Named for a nearby village, Vimy Ridge offered a clear view over much of the lowlands of Flanders. The Germans had to be removed before a planned Allied attack across the plain could succeed, yet three attempts by French forces had failed to dislodge them from their trenches, tunnels and pillboxes and resulted in enormous losses.

A surprise attack was impossible so the Canadian in charge of planning the operation, Major General Arthur Currie, insisted on weeks of training and meticulous preparation. Currie was

Canadians of the 29th Infantry Battalion (below and middle) advancing across 'No Man's Land' toward Vimy Ridge on the morning of April 9, 1917. In the photograph on the far right, the Canadians have reached the German lines and are searching the enemy trenches.

In this dramatic photograph (below), shells burst over Canadian troops digging in on Vimy Ridge on the afternoon of April 9, 1917. Meticulous preparation and a staggeringly effective artillery barrage had allowed the Canadians to take the previously impregnable German position, at a cost of 3,000 dead.

National Archives of Canada

determined to avoid a repetition of the futile battles on the Somme, which in two months had cost the Corps more than 26,000 dead and wounded. Vimy would be the first time all four Canadian divisions would fight together in an attack planned by their own officers. Success was seen as a matter of national pride. Through a bitterly cold winter the Canadians practised their assault on a replica of the Vimy battlefield built behind Allied lines. They would assault the ridge in small groups rather than the usual massed ranks of infantry, but the key to success lay in the ability of artillery and infantry to work together. If the shelling stopped before the infantry were virtually on top of the German positions, the enemy would emerge from their deep fortifications, man their machine guns and there would be a repeat of earlier slaughters. Timing was everything.

Supported by a thunderous artillery barrage from more than 3,000 Canadian and British guns, the Canadian Corps attacked the ridge at daybreak on April 9 and by 11:15 a.m. had

National Archives of Canada

National Archives of Canada

reached the top. The savage battle continued for four days, but finally the Germans were pushed out of their formerly impregnable positions. Entire German battalions were wiped out and thousands of prisoners and hundreds of artillery pieces were captured in what the French government called "an Easter gift from Canada to France." It was a rare and spectacular victory in a war of grinding attrition. The Canadians captured more ground at Vimy than British forces had taken in the previous two and a half years of fighting, and British, French and American newspapers hailed the battle as a triumph for Canada.

The triumph came with a heavy price - 7,000 casualties, 3,598 dead - but in the Great War success was relative. The futile French attempts to take the same ridge during 1915 had resulted in 150,000 casualties. In acknowledgement of the debt owed to the Canadians, France gave the land atop Vimy Ridge to be "a part of Canada forever." The 250-acre memorial park is now part of Canada's national park system and contains one of the most stunning and moving of the many Great War monuments in Europe. Walter Allward's massive, soaring twin pillars are all the more impressive for having been built with money donated by thousands of grateful Canadians.

The assault at Vimy rapidly took on legendary status in Canada as the battle which turned a colony into an independent nation. In the later decades of the 20th century the liberal intelligentsia would portray the country's martial exploits as more regrettable than heroic as part of an attempt to instil pacifism and multiculturalism as the nation's core values. Yet the fact that the

Canadian soldiers on the top of Vimy Ridge (below), looking down on the shattered village of Vimy. The top of the escarpment afforded a panoramic view across the Douai plain and the lowlands of Flanders.

A group of weary Canadians takes shelter in the remains of a German machine gun emplacement on Vimy Ridge. The German troops had been in possession of the ridge for almost three years, and had been well dug in.

Great War was marked by a lack of effective leadership and a shocking waste of life (two truths which would certainly not have been disputed by the soldiers who actually fought it) surely makes the performance of the Canadian Corps at Vimy all the more remarkable. In that war it stands as a rare example of an operation marked by intelligence, effective organization and the co-operative involvement of the men who would do the actual fighting. As author James Scott (*Canada At War And Peace*, Esprit de Corps Books, Ottawa, 2000) has described it, Vimy was "one bright feature on a vast landscape of futility."

As a metaphor for Canadian nationhood, Vimy was (and remains) proof that Canadians

can make an important contribution to world events and earn the respect of other nations. Canadians had proved themselves innovative, courageous and capable of outperforming the great powers of the Old World. For the young country it was a tremendous confidence booster and some consolation for the dreadful experience of Flanders. In the more cynical parlance of later times, it might be said Vimy created a myth in which all Canadians could believe - except in this case the "myth" was substantially fact.

Unfortunately, the lessons of Vimy were not absorbed by the Allied high command. Perhaps because it was only a part of what became known as the Second Battle of the Aisne, the success of the Canadians did not translate into a wider victory as British troops once more assaulted the German lines in Flanders - with the usual appalling loss of life for little gain.

The battle for the lowlands of Flanders dragged on through the summer of 1917, with the Canadian Corps - now commanded by a Canadian, the recently knighted Sir Arthur Currie - in the thick of the action around the town of Lens. Among the German troops they had gained a reputation as a fierce and ruthless enemy. They had become masters of the "trench raid," appearing by surprise in enemy lines and wreaking havoc before disappearing as quickly as they had arrived. The raids were calculated to spread fear among German troops (which they certainly did), but they also produced anger and resentment. There were reports of some captured Canadians being shot and others denied medical treatment by German doctors.

In October the Canadians were back in the Ypres Salient (a huge bulge in the Allied line) for an assault on another strategic ridge - this one near the village of Passchendaele. Arthur Currie was sceptical from the beginning. The terrain, mostly reclaimed marshland, was difficult to cross and the enemy well dug in on the high ground. "Let the Germans have it," he told Field Marshal Sir Douglas Haig, the British commander in chief. "It isn't worth a drop of blood." He argued that any assault across the waterlogged battlefield, criss-crossed by creeks and dotted with ponds, could result in 16,000 casualties. But Haig was insistent. Supported by the Australian and New Zealand Corps (the ANZACS) to the south and British troops to the north, the Canadians would spearhead the assault on Passchendaele Ridge.

With less than two weeks preparation (which

Haig thought too long and Currie considered not nearly long enough), the Canadians attacked on October 26. Torrential rain and millions of shells turned the battlefield into a quagmire and produced the most awful conditions in an awful war. The clay mud, in places waist deep, was a cloying, pitiless enemy almost as deadly as the crack German regiments the Canadians faced. Many of the wounded simply disappeared into the mud and were never found.

Fighting from trench to trench, the Canadians reached their last objective on November 10 and the assault ground to a halt. Four days later the haggard and mud-encrusted remnants of the Corps were relieved. Despite the usual predictions of an easy victory, British casualties in the four-month struggle for the Ypres Salient numbered around 325,000. Among them were 16,000 Canadians killed and wounded at Passchendaele. Currie's prediction had been accurate.

The slaughter shook even Prime Minister Borden's stern commitment to the war. At the time it seemed the battle had produced few

Triumphant Canadian troops returning from Vimy (below), and a game of cards enjoyed in a shell hole after the battle (opposite page). The first entirely Canadian operation of the war, Vimy was one bright spot in a conflict noted for futility and senseless slaughter.

Photos - National Archives of Canada

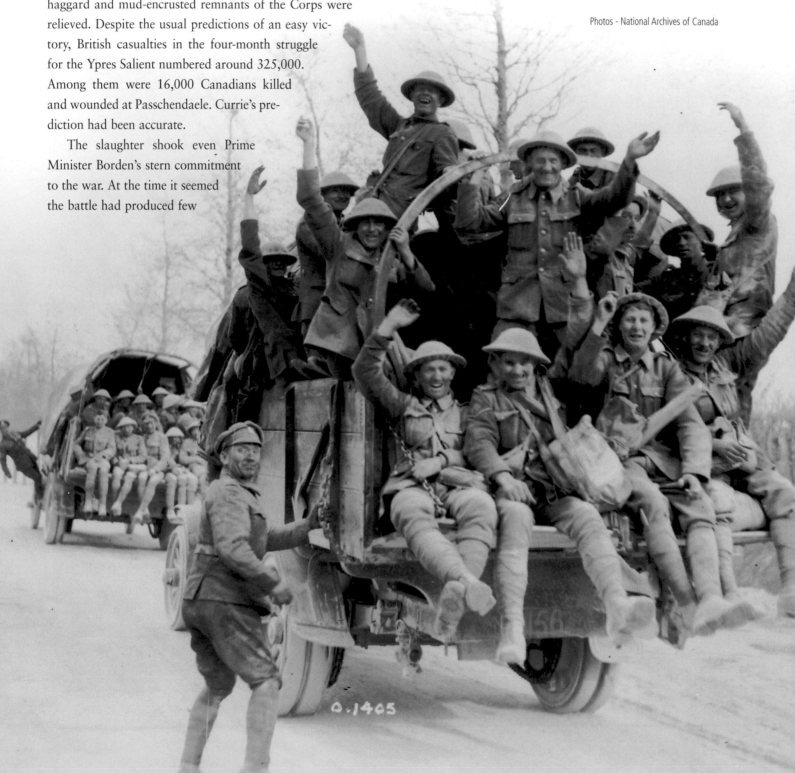

strategic gains and had been another costly paper victory. By the spring of 1918, the Passchendaele Ridge would, in fact, be back in Germans hands after British troops withdrew with hardly a fight. Yet after the war it became clear from the reports of German commanders that the Canadian-led Allied offensive in the fall of 1917 had fatally damaged German morale and fighting ability. Gen. Hermann von Kuhl judged it to be the turning point of the war: "The Flanders battle wore down the German strength to a degree at which the damage could not be repaired."

After Passchendaele Currie was forced to fight off a serious attempt to either break up the Canadian Corps to reinforce British units, or expand it into a two-corps army with six divisions. Expansion would likely have meant a promotion for Currie, but he had worked hard to build the Corps into the most effective formation among the Allied armies and he wasn't about to see it

Arthur Currie

The Teacher Who Became Canada's Greatest General

Aportly former teacher and realtor, Arthur Currie was not, perhaps, the most likely candidate to make a superb battlefield general. Yet the meticulous and, above all, practical Canadian became the most innovative and successful Allied commander of the Great War and arguably the only truly great general his country has ever produced.

Raised in Strathroy, Ontario, the six-foot-four-inch Currie was a militia officer in Vancouver when he was appointed as a brigade commander with the first Canadian troops to go overseas in 1914. He was as green as his troops when he led them into battle at Ypres the following April, but Currie learned quickly and gained confidence. By September he was in command of the 1st Division.

Currie had a firmer grasp than most of the complexities of this new style of warfare, which made planning and organization as important as courage and daring. In marked contrast to many of his fellow generals and the Allied high command, he didn't consider troops expendable. He was convinced that victory would go to the army which made the best use of its resources and manpower, and he encouraged officers who thought the same way.

In the winter of 1916-17 Currie was given the leading role in planning the attack on Vimy Ridge. Well aware of the terrible losses incurred by the French in attempting to take the same objective in 1915, he studied the French operation and insisted on painstaking preparation. The successful attack on April 9, 1917, was the most decisive British victory of the war to that point, and Currie pronounced it "the grandest day the Corps ever had." On June 1 he was knighted by King George V, and a week later he took over from Gen. Sir Julian Byng as the first Canadian commander of the Corps.

With Currie's promotion, Sam Hughes (no longer a cabinet minister but still a powerful voice in Ottawa) lobbied for the appointment of his son, Garnet, as commander of the 1st Division. Although he owed his original appointment to the father, Currie would have none of it. He had served with Garnet Hughes and had not been impressed. Incensed, father and son began a campaign to vilify and undermine Currie which would last until well after the war and ultimately tarnish the reputation of Canada's greatest general.

As commander of the Canadian Corps, Currie gathered around him a group of talented officers and fostered a series of innovations which would, quite literally, change the conduct of modern warfare. Lt.-Col. Andrew McNaughton (later to be the Canadian Army commander in the Second World War, used science to improve the accuracy of artillery and introduced new tactics designed "to pay the price of victory in shells, and not in the lives of men." Brigadier Bill Lindsay organized specialist brigades for engineering and construction, which left the infantry free to concentrate on fighting. Brigadier Ray Brutinel created the first mobile machine-gun battalions, mounting the guns in armoured cars (a move decades ahead of its time). The Canadians even had specialist intelligence officers to improve the accuracy and reliability of information. Currie was, in effect, breaking away from the tactical doctrine of the 19th century and professionalizing what had, until then, been the preserve of gentlemanly amateurs. Many of the innovations introduced by the Corps would later be adopted by the British and Americans, and eventually most other armies.

Currie fought to create a command structure based on merit and which worked, a rarity in that war. He brought together a group of experienced and trusted officers, British as well as Canadian, leaving the lesser lights with the (5th) reserve division in England (including the smouldering Garnet Hughes). Currie fought off attempts to break up the Corps and refused to dilute its efficiency by expanding it into a six-division army. He eventually agreed to a plan in which the 5th Division was broken up - but only after assurances it would be used to reinforce the existing Canadian Corps.

Under Currie's command, the Corps never lost a battle after Vimy and by the spring of 1918 its beefed-up battalions (each now had 100 additional infantry) had been moulded into four powerful 21,000-man divisions, each with its own engineers, artillery and mobile machine-gun companies. The Canadians were now regarded as crack troops by the Allied high command and feared by the Germans, who recognized Canadian movement into the line as a sure sign of an imminent assault. Currie was so highly regarded by British Prime Minister Lloyd George that he favoured the Canadian as overall commander of British forces in France - which was unthinkable from the perspective of the rigidly class-conscious British generals. But had the war continued into 1919, Lloyd George might have had his way.

In recognition of his own achievements and the central role of the Canadian Corps in the final Allied assault during the

summer and fall of 1918, Currie led the 1st and 2nd Divisions across the Rhine at the head of the British occupation forces. It was one of the few public acknowledgements Currie would receive. He returned home quietly in 1919 and became principal and vice-chancellor at McGill University. In typical Canadian fashion, there was little official recognition for the man who had been the most successful Allied general of the war. The British government awarded Field Marshal Haig $240,000 and gave him a peerage. The government in Ottawa considered a similar grant for Currie, but thought better of it.

Much worse, his reputation was under attack by the vindictive Sam Hughes, who used his privileged position in the House of Commons to claim Currie had needlessly sacrificed the lives of his men in the capture of Mons in the final days of the war. It was a ludicrous charge. Mons had been almost undefended and taken without serious casualties. In a war marked by appalling loss of life Currie had championed careful planning and innovative tactics in an effort to limit losses. Several of the general's former comrades came to his defence yet no member of the government bothered to officially refute the charges or support Currie. For almost a decade the allegations hung over him like a cloud, and as a result they were believed by many - even some veterans of the Corps.

Finally, in 1927 (after Sam Hughes' death) the allegations appeared in a form which allowed Currie the right to a public defence. When a plaque was unveiled in Mons to commemorate the liberation of the city by the Canadian Corps, a front-page editorial in the *Port Hope Evening Guide*, an Ontario weekly newspaper, repeated the charges made by Hughes eight years earlier and Currie immediately sued for defamation.

The editorial, written by local Liberal activist W.T.R. Preston, alleged "it is doubtful whether there was a more deliberate and useless waste of human life than in the so-called capture of Mons." The case made headlines across the country, which was clearly Currie's hope. Under cross-examination he explained his decision to sue. "It [the editorial] holds me up before the people of this country as a murderer, a man who didn't exercise due regard for the lives of the men under him. If that is true, I do not deserve to be a general; I do not deserve to be principal of McGill. In fact, I am charged with a crime that is punishable."

The trial lasted for two weeks, during which the general's reputation was put through the grinder. Garnet Hughes fed the newspaper's lawyers with every rumour and item of gossip which had ever attached to Currie, all of which were duly reported across the country (and would continue to resurface for decades to come). The treatment was so savage that public opinion began to swing heavily in Currie's favour.

In his charge to the jury, the judge noted that no Canadian had been killed at Mons. The jury returned a verdict in Currie's favour and awarded him token damages of $500. There was

Arthur Currie in 1917. He moulded the Canadian Corps into the most effective fighting force on the Western Front.

General Currie with Field Marshal Sir Douglas Haig. If the war had dragged on into 1919, the former B.C. teacher and real-tor might well have replaced Haig in overall command of the Allied armies.

widespread sympathy for the general and, at long last, belated public admiration for his achievements (a military band greet-ed his return to Montreal and he was feted at banquets and luncheons). But more importantly to Currie there was recogni-tion that he had not been reckless with the lives of his men.

The stressful trial had, however, taken its toll. When an appeal was launched two weeks after the trial, Currie collapsed. He would eventually win, but his health was permanently

impaired (he lived for some time on a diet of orange juice and milk) and he died of pneumonia in 1933 at the age of 57.

The names of many Great War generals - French, Haig, Ludendorff, Hindenburg, Joffre, Foch and Pershing live on. Some are reviled and others respected, but all are remembered in some manner by their fellow citizens. All except the best of them all - Arthur Currie, whose achievements have become mostly invisible to all but historians and soldiers. ■

Canadian soldiers mending shirts (above), May 1917. The bulk of a soldier's time was actually spent behind the front lines, training or attending to routine tasks that were difficult or impossible in the mud of the trenches.

dismantled or weakened by expansion, which he viewed as unnecessary and unwarranted. The issue brought to a head his long-running disagreements with Haig. Currie took his case to the Canadian and British governments. Borden stood by his general, and Currie also found he had a supporter in Lloyd George, who had doubts about his own high command. The Corps would not be broken up, and the 5th Division (still in reserve in England) would be used to reinforce Currie's four divisions in France.

Haig, an aristocratic cavalry officer and scion of the famous Scottish distillery family, was outraged at this challenge to his authority. He accused Currie of insubordination, and wondered "if some people in Canada regard themselves rather as 'allies' than fellow citizens of the Empire?"

That was, of course, precisely how they regarded themselves.

Away from the front, British Prime Minister David Lloyd George had persuaded the Imperial War Cabinet - which included Robert Borden - that since America had finally entered the war (in the spring of 1917), fresh troops and a final big push by the Allies could bring a rapid end to the dreadful conflict. Borden was convinced and promised substantial

Cheery displays of "trench warfare" (opposite left) were staged by military units across the country, but by 1916, with Canadian losses approaching 35,000, even civilians were beginning to comprehend the awful reality of the war. A British tank (above), the new wonder weapon of the war, puts on a demonstration in Toronto.

Photos - National Archives of Canada

Canadian reinforcements. Yet back home the pool of willing volunteers was almost dry and it was a promise he could not fulfill without resorting to conscription. That would mean a political fight and overwhelming opposition in Quebec and among farmers. If the victory at Vimy had united Canadians as never before, the bitter argument over conscription would once again divide the country.

Despite government censorship and media cheerleading, the Canadian public by now had some understanding of the brutal reality of the war. It would be years before the public would learn how close the Germans had come to choking off the lifeline across the North Atlantic (U-boats had even managed to operate in the Gulf of St. Lawrence), but there was no hiding the scale of the conflict or the appalling losses. Scandals over the procurement of war supplies did nothing to bolster public confidence in the conduct of the war, and the popularity of the Borden government was at a low ebb. Defeatism was shunned, to be sure, but the original enthusiasm for the war had faded.

That was particularly true among French Canadians, who were upset by the lack of French units and who were in any case less susceptible to calls for British solidarity. Across the country, many farmers also resisted the notion of conscription, arguing - with some justification - that if the

country and its soldiers wanted to eat, their need for manpower was as great as that of the army.

Fearing its impact on the war effort, both Borden and Laurier tried to avoid a political confrontation over conscription. Borden proposed a coalition with the Liberals for the duration of the war: He offered half the positions in a coalition cabinet, led by Borden, in return for Liberal support in the House of Commons to enact conscription. Laurier himself supported the war effort and understood that public opinion and most of his own English-speaking

The Victory Bond campaign (above) generated close to $2 billion from patriotic Canadians during the war years. The ability to raise so much capital from within the country came as a revelation to the federal government.

National Archives of Canada

MPs would support a coalition government, but in 1914 he had promised Quebeckers that Canada would send only volunteers overseas. Laurier would not now go back on his word. He refused Borden's offer and suggested, instead, a national referendum - which the prime minister had rejected as too divisive. Borden had little choice but to use his parliamentary majority to pass a conscription law, and in August became a reality for all single men between the ages of 20 and 32.

The clergy and virtually all political leaders in Quebec opposed a draft and urged Quebeckers to resist. Others did more than resist and the homes of a prominent senator and the owner of the Montreal *Star* were bombed. Throughout the summer and fall of 1917 there were violent demonstrations against conscription in Montreal and Quebec City that resulted in sev-

Canadian artillery in action (left) at Angres, France. In the build-up to Vimy, Andrew McNaughton, a young scientist from McGill University, was given the task of making the Canadian Corps' guns more mobile and effective, particularly at taking out enemy artillery. He succeeded brilliantly, silencing 70% of the German artillery positions before the infantry charged the Vimy escarpment. Tanks waiting to go into action in support of Canadian infantry (below). By 1918 the Canadian Corps had combined armour, mobile artillery, and rifle platoons into a new style of warfare that made them the elite troops of the British Expeditionary Force.

Photos - National Archives of Canada

eral deaths. Many young men took to the woods rather than report to the recruitment office.

Against this background of bitterness and division, Borden was forced to call a general election (already delayed once) in December. With the Liberals split on conscription, the outcome was never really in doubt. A vote against the government, it was claimed, was a vote against reinforcements to support Canadians fighting and dying in Europe. It was a vote for defeat. It was disloyal. Nevertheless, Borden took no chances. A Wartime Election Act was quickly passed which disenfranchised any immigrant from an enemy country who had arrived in Canada after 1900; the majority of whom were Liberal supporters. Special arrangements were made so that Canadians serving overseas could vote, and for the first time military nurses and women with immediate family serving in Europe (husbands, fathers, sons) were allowed to vote. Towards the end of the campaign, just to be sure, Borden also promised the farming lobby they would get their exemption from conscription.

Borden's new coalition of Conservatives and pro-conscription Liberals won almost 60 per

cent of the popular vote and 153 of the 235 seats in the Commons. But the cost had been a return to the bitter French-English animosities of the past. Canada's linguistic divide was yawning dangerously again, and as 1918 dawned Borden was aware that victory had to be swift or the political consequences for the country might be worse than the war itself.

In the spring of 1918 the Allied and German armies faced each other across the same battlefields they had fought over during three and a half years of murderous conflict. America's entry into the war promised an end to the bloody stalemate and U.S. troops were finally arriving in France. But, as is often the case with bad situations, first things got worse. With the collapse of the Russian government in 1917, the Germans had been able to transfer thousands of troops to the Western Front. Now they launched a last, desperate attempt to bring about a decisive battlefield victory before more troops arrived from North America. Germany's leaders accepted that the war could not be won but they wanted to enter peace negotiations from a position of strength.

The attack caught the Allies unprepared. Haig's staff had pronounced the Germans incapable of

The utter desolation of Passchendaele, Belgium (right). Canadian soldiers carrying duckboards (below) to cross the mud and water-filled shell holes - which were as lethal as enemy fire. Over British opposition, the Canadians built their own sawmill to manufacture the walkways - which were rapidly copied by other Allied armies.

National Archives of Canada

launching such an offensive. Suddenly the possibility of a German victory looked very real and the need for reinforcements was critical. Borden decided to break his promise to Canadian farmers. Their sons would not be exempt from conscription after all. That didn't stop them, and most others, from applying for exemptions. More than 90 per cent of draftees did just that. In the end it was Canada's cities, primarily in southern Ontario, which provided most of the conscripts. In Quebec and across the farmlands of Ontario and the Prairies, local authorities adopted a liberal attitude to exemptions and few were drafted who were unwilling to go. All told, 100,000 men were drafted for the war's final act, and almost 50,000 Canadian reinforcements were shipped to England in 1918. About half of them would see action, fighting alongside the volunteer veterans of the Canadian Corps - who often treated the reluctant rookies with disdain.

Canadian nurses in France (below) vote in the 1917 federal election, the first in which a limited number of women were allowed to vote (if they were serving with the armed forces, or had a close male relative on active service). For Prime Minister Robert Borden (pictured above right with his wife, Laura), the vote produced a decisive victory for his coalition government - but at the cost of deep divisions across the country.

Photos - National Archives of Canada

Robert Borden and Winston Churchill at an Imperial Conference in London. Borden began the war as a staunch Imperialist, but after the debacle of Passchendaele the quiet Nova Scotian is said to have grabbed British Prime Minister Lloyd George by the lapels and warned that if such a thing happened again "not a Canadian soldier will leave the shores of Canada so long as the Canadian people trust the government of their country to me." Lloyd George was apparently impressed.

The Big Bang

An Atomic-Size Explosion
Levels The City Of Halifax

At the end of 1917 Canada had been at war for three and a half years and had suffered tens of thousands of casualties on the battlefields of Belgium and France. As if that were not enough, the country was suddenly hit with the largest civilian disaster in its history.

At 8:40 a.m. on the morning of December 6, the French freighter *Mont Blanc* was entering Halifax harbour through The Narrows carrying 5,000 tons of explosives in its hold and a deck cargo of flammable benzol. Originating in New York, the *Mont Blanc* was to join a convoy before heading overseas. Leaving the harbour at the same time was the Norwegian cargo vessel *Imo*, carrying medicine and humanitarian supplies for refugee camps in Belgium.

Witnesses later reported that as the ships closed on each other, there was a sudden and rapid exchange of whistles and signals between them. Moments later, the bow of the *Imo* ripped open the foredeck of the *Mont Blanc*, allowing thousands of gallons of benzol to pour down on to the contents of the hold.

A blue flame began creeping through the swirling fumes escaping from the *Mont Blanc's* damaged hull. Suspecting an explosion was imminent, the captain of the *Imo* reversed his vessel away from the stricken freighter and headed at full speed across the harbour towards Dartmouth. The captain and crew of the *Mont Blanc*, acutely aware of their cargo, abandoned ship and began frantically rowing lifeboats across to the Dartmouth shore.

The crippled, smouldering *Mont Blanc*, now crewless, was left drifting towards the Halifax wharves. A crowd of some 200 people stopped to watch, while along the waterfront more people gathered as a horse-drawn fire engine, its bell ringing, clattered by. For twenty minutes, as sailors from nearby vessels tried to douse the blaze, smoke and flame poured from the bowels of the stricken ship. Few of those fighting the fire or watching from shore knew what was in the *Mont Blanc's* hold. Just before 9 a.m., the burning ship hit the end of Pier Six and set it ablaze.

As the *Mont Blanc's* crew took shelter behind a stand of trees on

the Dartmouth side of the harbour, their ship erupted in a white flash, accompanied moments later by what one survivor called "the clap of doom." The *Mont Blanc* and the men fighting the fire disappeared. Within 800 metres of the blast almost everything, including thousands of tons of water, was vapourized by a terrific blast of air superheated to 5,000 degrees C. Within 1.5 kilometres, buildings were ripped apart or flattened and huge chunks of debris were hurled into the city. The explosion momentarily exposed the seabed and a wave more than six metres high swept through the streets of Halifax and Dartmouth - and then just as rapidly retreated, sucking hundreds of people with it to drown in the roiling, debris-filled waters of the harbour.

Within a few minutes 2,000 lives had been extinguished, 9,000 people injured and 25,000 left homeless. Until the nuclear bomb dropped on Hiroshima, it was the largest man-made explosion in history. Houses shook in Sydney, over 300 kilometres away, and tremors could be felt as far away as New England. The following day, as people tried to find loved ones and picked through the wreckage of their homes, it began to snow and a week-long blizzard closed over the shattered city.

Volunteers and supplies poured in from across Canada and the United States, while Halifax's military garrison swung into action to aid the civilian authorities. Hospitals across Nova Scotia were packed with the seriously hurt, many suffering terrible burns or blinded or slashed by flying glass. When beds were filled, the injured were laid on the floor. For some, the tragedy was beyond bearing. One young doctor finished a lengthy shift tending the wounded, returned to his office and hanged himself.

There wasn't a school in Halifax left undamaged. The explosion had happened minutes after classes had begun and many children were among the dead and wounded. In the city's Protestant orphanage 200 children and staff were lost. Entire families were gone, and the loss of five, ten or more relatives was not uncommon. One survivor, 40-year-old Mary Jean Jackson, lost her husband, ten children, her mother, four brothers and two sisters. In all, 54 of her relatives perished. Another family in the working class district of Richmond, near the docks, lost 46, almost half of them children.

At first it was rumoured that the blast was the result of sabotage by German agents. The Halifax *Herald* proclaimed "that the prime responsibility for this rests with... that arch fiend, the Emperor of the Germans." In fact, no such plot existed. The crew of the *Mont Blanc* and most of the crew of the *Imo* had survived, so there was no lack of evidence about what had actually happened. A public inquiry found the captain and pilot of the *Mont Blanc* solely responsible for the tragedy and they were charged with manslaughter. The case eventually went to the Supreme Court of Canada, and later the British Privy Council, both of which found the two ships equally at fault for the accident. In the end, no one went to jail.

The 1917 explosion left deep scars on the memories of those who lived through it. Among the survivors was 10-year-old Hugh MacLennan, who in 1941 would publish *Barometer Rising*, his first novel and a moving account of a tragedy now almost lost in the greater horror of the First World War. ∎

The Halifax waterfront the day after the explosion. A scene of total devastation, with buildings reduced to matchwood.

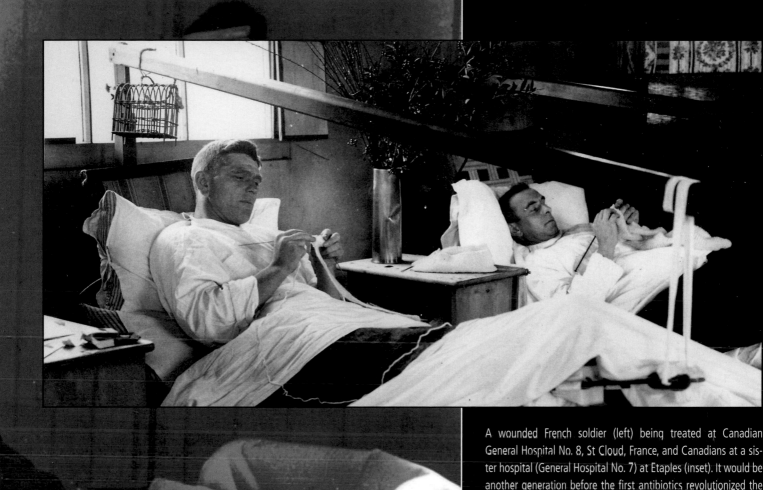

A wounded French soldier (left) being treated at Canadian General Hospital No. 8, St Cloud, France, and Canadians at a sister hospital (General Hospital No. 7) at Etaples (inset). It would be another generation before the first antibiotics revolutionized the treatment of wounds, but hospitals such as these represented a huge step forward in the treatment of casualties.

Photos - National Archives of Canada

Billy Bishop

A Young Canadian With An Attitude
Becomes The Allies' Top Fighter Ace

O f all the Canadian heroes of the Great War, none has been more enduring or controversial than William Avery Bishop. In fact, repeated attempts to discredit Bishop kept his name in the public eye throughout the 20th century and beyond.

Born in Owen Sound, Ontario, Billy Bishop was known as a young man who cared little for authority, rules and regulations. He was trouble. Not exactly a budding member of Canada's Edwardian establishment, but perhaps the perfect candidate for the dare-devil life of a Royal Flying Corps' pilot.

Bishop was an accomplished rider and handy with a rifle, so he tried to join a cavalry regiment at the outbreak of war. Sidelined by pneumonia, he instead joined the RFC as an observer while recovering in England. It took him more than a year to get accepted for

pilot training but his persistence finally paid off, and to say he took to his new life as a pilot is an understatement: He was a natural flyer and less than a month after joining 60 Squadron in France he registered three "kills" in one day and became an official ace.

The main complaint against Bishop was that he embellished his combat reports. Accurate confirmation was often difficult to obtain, but this was a fact of life for all pilots - not just Bishop. The precise number of aircraft he shot down may be open to dispute - it might have been a few more or less than the 75 he is credited with - but there is no doubt that Bishop was courageous and deadly in combat and accounted for a large number of enemy planes. The Germans were sure enough of his reputation to put a price on his head.

In June 1917 Bishop was awarded the Victoria Cross for a lone early morning attack on a German airfield at Estourmel,

Captain Billy Bishop at the controls of his RFC Sopwith Camel aircraft. Pneumonia prevented the war's greatest fighter pilot from joining the cavalry.

France, in which he was credited with destroying three enemy aircraft. The unauthorized mission was the first pre-emptive strike on an enemy airfield and his actions were immediately controversial. Defended with anti-aircraft guns, airfields had been considered too dangerous a target for the relatively slow-moving planes of the time. Bishop proved otherwise.

The fact that some details of the attack could not be independently confirmed would be used again and again in attempts to discredit Bishop (even in 1917 there was no shortage of those who were eager to knock the cocky Canadian off his perch), but there can be no question of the bravery and skill of a pilot who had already demonstrated both on many occasions. ∎

A signed photograph of Billy Bishop, taken in the summer of 1917, and Nanaimo, B.C.'s Raymond Collishaw (above) with his squadron at Allonville, France, a year later. Some 12,000 Canadians served with the Royal Flying Corps and its successor, the Royal Air Force. By some counts Collishaw had more enemy "kills" to his credit than Bishop, and he went on to a long and distinguished career in the RAF, retiring with the rank of Air Vice-Marshal.

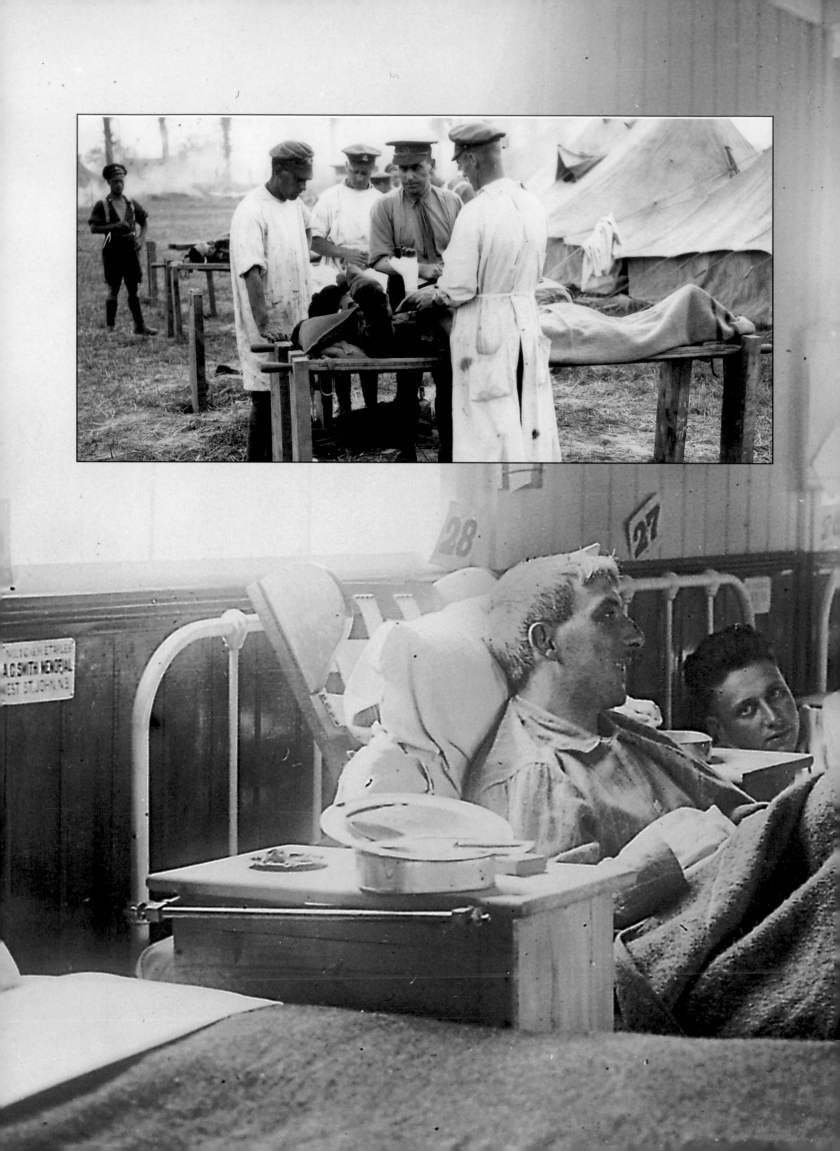

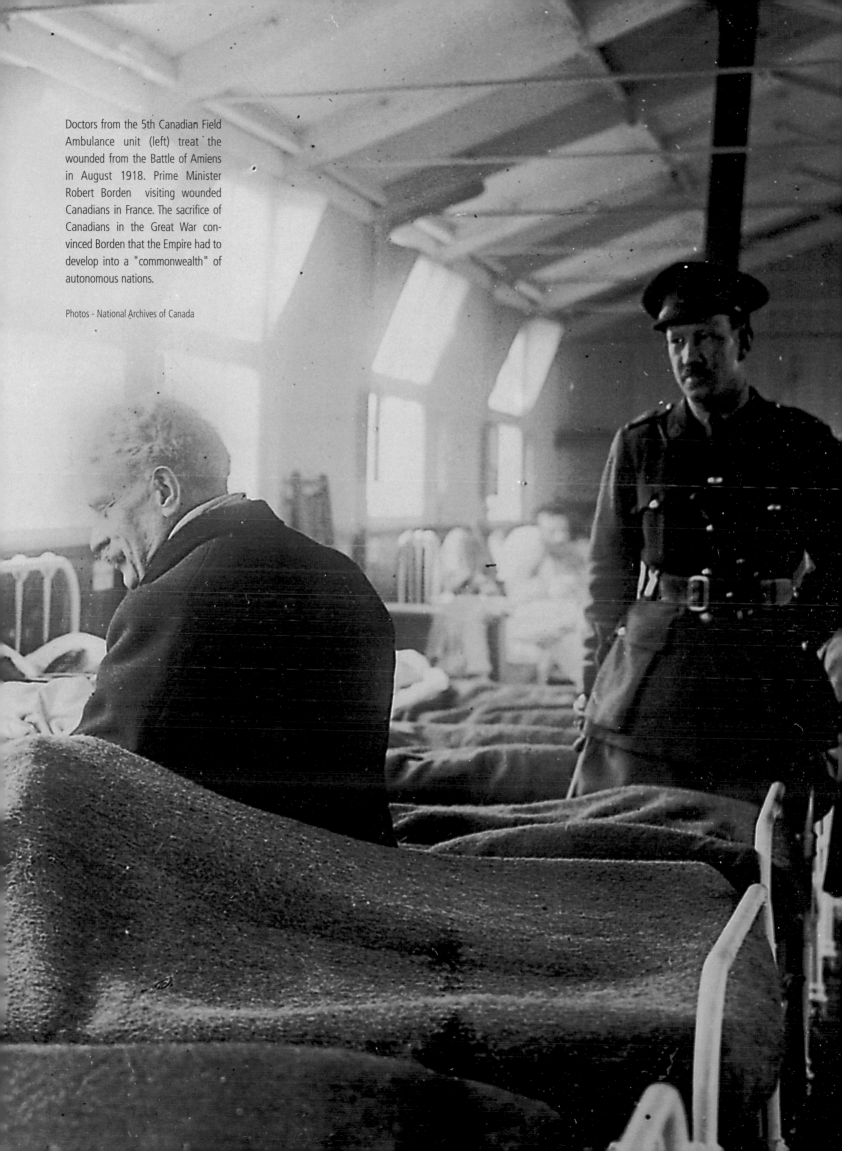

Doctors from the 5th Canadian Field Ambulance unit (left) treat the wounded from the Battle of Amiens in August 1918. Prime Minister Robert Borden visiting wounded Canadians in France. The sacrifice of Canadians in the Great War convinced Borden that the Empire had to develop into a "commonwealth" of autonomous nations.

Nurses lay wreaths at the grave of Nursing Sister Margaret Lowe in the Canadian war cemetery at Etaples, France. Hospitals and dressing stations were not immune from German attack.

The German offensive of 1918, Operation Michael, involved 76 divisions (close to a million troops), supported by 7,000 artillery pieces and 700 aircraft. The attack began on the morning of March 21st along a 40-mile front and over the next nine days the Germans were able to gain more ground than at any time since 1914. The British Fifth Army was virtually destroyed and Allied troops were pushed back to the River Avre a few miles from the vital railway junction of Amiens. From there German artillery was able to shell the outskirts of Paris. These were Germany's first major territorial gains in almost four years, but the effort exhausted the supply of troops and munitions. The assault slowed and then stopped.

The British began a counteroffensive on August 8, with the Canadian and Australian Corps forming the spearhead of the Allied attack. After three months of training under Currie's new

A funeral (below) at Doullens, France, in May 1918, for three Canadian nurses and two doctors killed in an air raid on the 3rd Stationary Hospital.

National Archives of Canada

Rifle Wood

Canada's Horsemen Ride Into History

Outside the tiny French village of Moreuil, on March 30, 1918, the Canadian Cavalry Brigade launched one of the few cavalry charges of the Great War and helped repel the massive German offensive known as Operation Michael.

Over the previous week the German forces had rolled up the British Fifth Army and advanced to within a few kilometres of the strategic rail junction of Amiens. One more push and the Kaiser's forces could have seriously damaged the Allies' ability to move in reinforcements and supplies by train, and Paris would have been within range of the German artillery.

When the Canadians arrived on the scene, German infantry supported by machine guns and artillery were occupying a wooded ridge overlooking Moreuil and its strategic river crossing.

The cavalry was ordered to prevent the German troops from securing the wood. The Royal Canadian Dragoons attacked from the west and south, driving out hundreds of German troops. Two squadrons were cut to pieces charging the enemy machine guns and field artillery, and the rest of the regiment, joined by troopers of the Fort Garry Horse, dismounted and began to fight its way through the wood on foot.

While the fighting continued, the brigade's third regiment - Lord Strathcona's Horse (Royal Canadians) - tried to outflank the Germans on the north side of the wood. Two squadrons of the Strathconas dismounted and attacked on foot while C Squadron, led by 33-year-old Lieutenant Gordon Flowerdew, was ordered around the northeast tip of the wood to prevent German reinforcements entering from that side. As Flowerdew, a British Columbia rancher, and his 75 troopers rounded the corner of the wood they found the highway to the south packed with German reinforcements moving towards Moreuil. In an instant Flowerdew decided to sound the charge.

Unfortunately the Germans had been alerted to the possibility of an attack and five infantry companies, a machine company and a six-gun artillery battery had been deployed in front of the Strathconas. As the Canadians, swords drawn, began their charge they were about a thousand metres from the German artillery. Many, including Flowerdew, were cut down in the first seconds, but the rest thundered on towards the German infantry. In little more than a minute, most of the Canadian cavalrymen were dead or wounded. Only one horse and two wounded troopers reached the German guns. Of the 75 who had begun the charge, two dozen were killed outright and another fifteen, including Lt. Flowerdew, would die later of their

The Canadian Light Horse ride into action at Vimy, April 1917. The fact that cavalry were used at all in a war of machine guns and fighter aircraft owed much to the fact that many senior officers in the Allied high command were former cavalrymen themselves.

wounds. But the German advance faltered.

The Cavalry Brigade now occupied most of Moreuil Wood. Despite ferocious, hand to hand fighting against more heavily armed German forces, the Canadians held them off through the night until they were relieved by British infantry.

The fighting around what became known to the Canadians as Rifle Wood continued for several months, but the German forces would advance no farther. The desperate attempt to force an end to the conflict on German terms had failed, in no small measure due to the courage of the Canadian horsemen.

Rifle Wood was not the last Canadian cavalry charge. Four months later, as the Allies began their final, and ultimately victorious, offensive, the Brigade led a dramatic charge by the British 3rd Cavalry Division on the German lines around Beaucourt-en-Santerre, east of Amiens. It was one of the last cavalry actions of the war and one infantryman who witnessed it called it "the most glorious sight I'd ever seen." Like a scene from another age, the ground trembled and the air was filled with the thunder of hooves.

The reality was that the attack, like so many others in the new era of mechanized warfare, failed to achieve its objectives despite the incredible courage of men and horses in the face of machine guns and artillery. At Beaucourt the Canadian Brigade had far outdistanced the plodding new tanks guarding its flanks, but the machines were a sign of things to come. The cavalry, for so long the dashing elite of the battlefield, would soon exchange their horses for tanks and armoured vehicles, and the charge of the horsemen would pass into history. ∎

National Archives of Canada

A sign of things to come (below). Canadian cavalry training with machine guns, August 1917. The horsemen often saw more action as dismounted infantry than they did aboard their mounts.

National Archives of Canada

Giving first aid to a wounded Canadian cavalryman near Arras in September 1918. The horses were much faster than the plodding tanks that often accompanied them, but it was the cavalry's last hurrah.

doctrine of mobility and close artillery support, and reinforcement from the reserve division in England, the Canadians were the most formidable formation in the Allied armies. The supreme commander, French General Foch, called them "second to none," and over the coming months they were to prove him correct.

In three days the Canadians advanced 22 kilometres and took thousands of prisoners. Even the *London Times* conceded that the attack had been "chiefly a Canadian battle." A remarkable ten Victoria Crosses were won by Canadians in the fighting. Over the next few weeks, from Arras to the Canal du Nord, Cambrai, Valenciennes and Mons, the Canadians led the attack in what would become known as their "Hundred Days." It is one of the most remarkable records in modern warfare. As the German high command threw what was left of their army into a last-ditch effort to halt the Allies, the four divisions of the Canadian Corps faced and defeated a quarter of all the enemy soldiers in France (more than 50 divisions). The cost was terrible, almost 46,000 Canadian dead and wounded, but it forced Germany into peace negotiations and the end was finally in sight.

That didn't mean the fighting ended, but everywhere German resistance was collapsing. The Canadian Corps took Valenciennes on November 1, and by the night of the 10th they had reached the ruined city of Mons, Belgium, where the original British Expeditionary Force had first

Canadian troops playing cards (below) during a lull in the action in the Battle of Amiens, August 1918. That month saw the beginning of the final Allied offensive of the war, with the Canadians advancing an astonishing 22 kilometres in three days.

National Archives of Canada

Canadian troops supported by an armoured car (right) during the Battle of Amiens. Canadian troops (below) advance through German shellfire outside Arras. During the final 100 days of the war the four divisions of the Canadian Corps faced and defeated 50 German divisions. It stands as one of the most remarkable records in modern warfare.

Photos - National Archives of Canada

seen action at the end of August 1914. Lt. Gen. Currie reported that his exhausted men were sharing their rations with the half-starved inhabitants.

A short distance beyond Mons, on the road to Brussels, a monument marks the first shot of the war by a British soldier. A mere twenty yards away, on the other side of the road, there is a small plaque marking the point reached by the Canadians on Armistice Day, November 11, 1918: The farthest point of the Allied advance after four years of bloody fighting which had cost the lives of thirteen million people. The last Canadian to die was killed nearby by a German sniper three minutes before the armistice took effect at 11 a.m.

The face of modern warfare (below). The Canadian Motor Machine Gun Brigade on the Arras-Cambrai road in September 1918. The Canadian use of mobile troops took soldiers out of the trenches and brought an end to static warfare.

National Archives of Canada

In Ottawa, the first Canadian city to receive the news, the quiet of early morning was broken by the ringing of church bells and the wail of factory sirens. Across the country there were parades, speeches and enormous relief. And there was pride. Canada had played its part, and it had been a significant one.

In Mons there was also celebration and relief that the nightmare was finally over, but the end of the fighting didn't mean the end of hardship. "I thought we would all get loaded and have

a hell of a party," remembered Pte. F.R. Hasse of Edmonton. "But when the end came we just sat around." They were tired, often hungry and ready to go home, but for many their soldiering wasn't quite over. In recognition of the part they had played in the final victory, the 1st and 2nd Canadian Divisions led the British occupation forces on the 170-mile march to the Rhine. On December 13, 1918, the 1st Division entered Cologne while the 2nd crossed the river at Bonn. They would spend almost two months in Germany before beginning the long trek home through Belgium and England.

It would be the end of May 1919 before most of the 349,000 Canadians overseas at the end of the war could be repatriated, and for many it was a long and frustrating winter spent in temporary barracks under threat from a deadly new form of influenza. Several thousand Canadians also went on to serve in Russia, as part of operations supporting anti-Bolshevik forces around Murmansk in the North and Vladivostok on Siberia's Pacific coast. A few served in an RAF squadron supporting a White Russian army in southern Russia, but by the summer of 1919 most of these, too, would be back home. After three years and eight months of combat, of the 629,636 Canadians who had served their country in "the war to end all wars," 59,544 were dead and 212,306 had been wounded, many losing limbs or suffering permanent disability.

Politically, the war had reopened the divisions between Quebec and the rest of the country. Conscription would become one more grievance to add to the province's historical bag-

Canadian troops enter Valenciennes (below) on November 1, 1918. General Currie had been ordered to conserve shells, but instead ordered up a massive artillery barrage. Shells were expendable, he told his superiors, while men's lives were not. A Pte. Lawrence of Brantford, Ontario (top right), was the final Canadian casualty of the war. The 17-year-old was wounded 15 minutes before the November 11 armistice. Canadians liberate Mons, Belgium (bottom right), on the last morning of the war.

Photos - National Archives of Canada

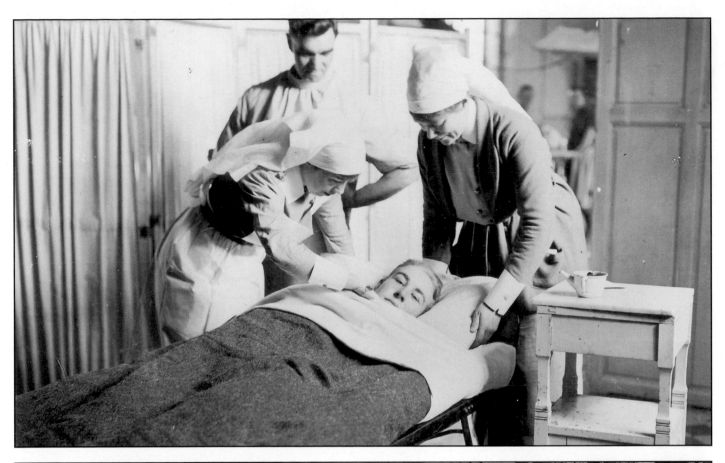

gage. Yet, in general, there's much truth in the claim that the Great War enhanced Canadians' growing sense of national identity.

In the trenches of northern France and Belgium a generation of young men from all corners of the country, all backgrounds and all walks of life became comrades and came to better know their nation through each other. The shared experiences of war, at home as well as in the army, united Canadians as never before. For the first time in the country's history it had faced the challenge of a protracted, nationwide effort which had involved almost every citizen in one way or another, and which had demanded terrible sacrifice. Begun as an obligation owed the mother country, the war had become a singular national achievement. By the most important yardstick of all, the perception of its citizens, Canada had entered the war as a colony and emerged from it a nation. ∎

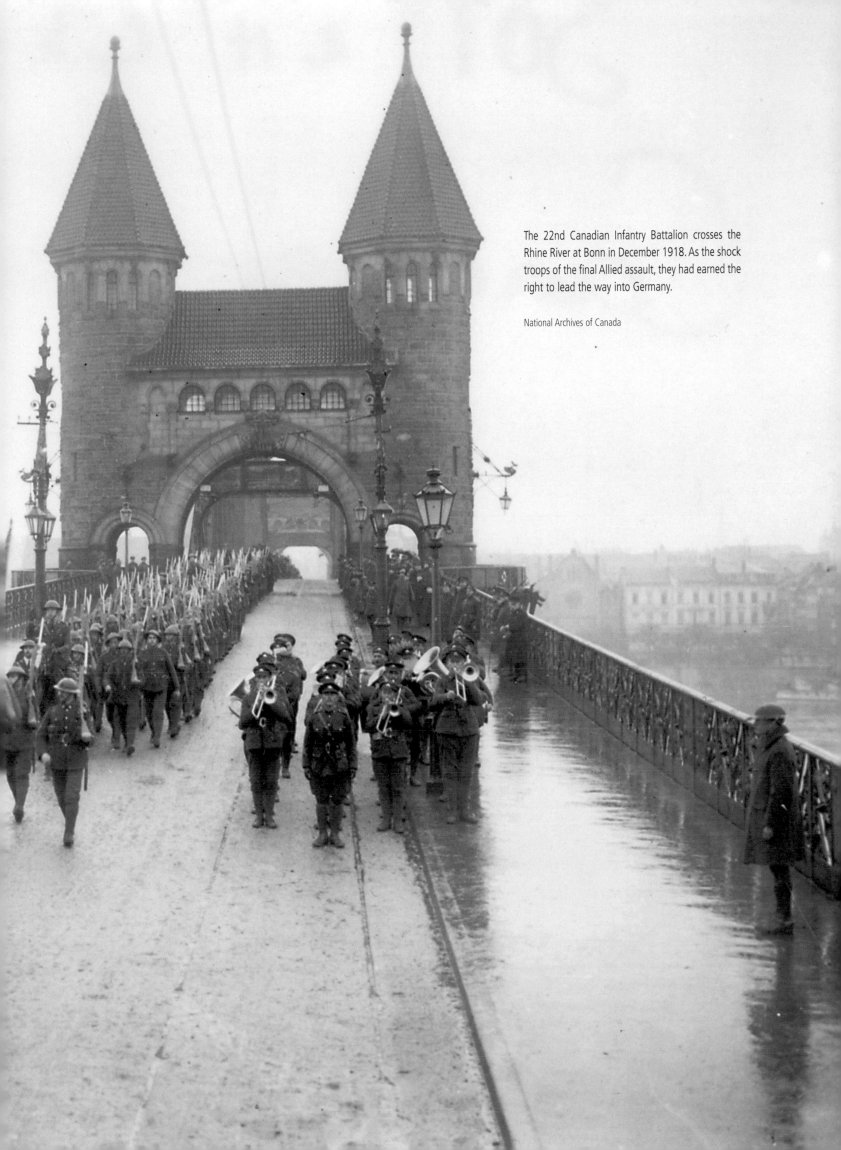

The 22nd Canadian Infantry Battalion crosses the Rhine River at Bonn in December 1918. As the shock troops of the final Allied assault, they had earned the right to lead the way into Germany.

National Archives of Canada

The troop ship *Olympic* docks in Halifax in early 1919 with a contingent of returning Canadian soldiers. It would be early summer before most of the Canadians returned home - and longer for some. The Canadian Siberian Expeditionary Force travelled from France to northern Russia to aid anti-Communist forces, but they, too, returned home in 1919. Several members of the expeditionary force are pictured below in Vladivostok.

Photos - National Archives of Canada

Walter Seymour Allward's stunning Vimy Memorial. In 1922 France donated the land for the battlefield park to the people of Canada for all time. The memorial itself was built with $1.5 million donated by Canadian citizens, and dedicated in 1936 by King Edward VIII in the presence of 50,000 French and Canadian war veterans and their families. It bears the names of 11,258 Canadian soldiers killed in the Great War.

The Spanish Influenza

A Killer More Deadly Than War

In the summer of 1918, after almost four years of war, the conflict in Europe seemed at long last to be turning in favour of Canada and its allies. The very last thing Canadians expected was the appearance of a new and deadly threat.

Since early in the year evidence of a new strain of influenza had been appearing in places as far apart as Kansas, China and Britain. The first published reports of people dying by the hundreds appeared in Spain, probably because it was not involved in the Great War and its media remained uncensored. As a result, even though the deadly outbreak didn't originate in Spain, it would go down in history as the Spanish Flu.

By the beginning of June the first wave of flu had made its appearance in Canada, carried by troops returning from the battlefields of France. By the end of the month most hospital ships docking at Canadian ports were reporting large numbers of soldiers suffering from an illness which began with cold-like symptoms followed by severe muscle cramps, aching and a high fever. Many men, already weakened by their injuries, quickly developed pneumonia and died. It seemed that the flu was another terrible consequence of the war and no great threat to a healthy civilian population.

But as infected soldiers returned to their homes across the country the disease began to appear among civilians in Quebec, Nova Scotia, and then Ontario. The authorities were slow to accept that something as seemingly minor as the flu or "grippe" could be so deadly. The Department of Defence announced that although the virus was contagious it "is not a serious one." Ontario's Board of Health rejected a call to close the province's schools on the grounds that there was no need to upset the public over something which would surely prove to be minor. Within a few weeks 100,000 schoolchildren in Toronto had become ill.

As fall turned into winter the disease spread from coast to coast and hundreds of thousands of people, many of them healthy young adults, became sick. Hospitals were overwhelmed. Healthcare had made enormous strides in the previous half century, but there were no antibiotics and it would be another fifteen years before the flu virus was identified. People turned to folk remedies, including onions, camphor, violet-leaf tea or even tobacco. Cigarettes and cigar sales boomed. Alcohol, too, was seen as potentially beneficial. It was still subject to prohibition but could be had from government liquor dispensaries with a doctor's prescription. The $2 prescriptions were so popular that dispensary line-ups could take hours.

Hotels, theatres, restaurants and dance halls stood empty or closed as the outbreak dragged on through the spring of 1919. Eventually the isolation of the sick and the use of gauze or

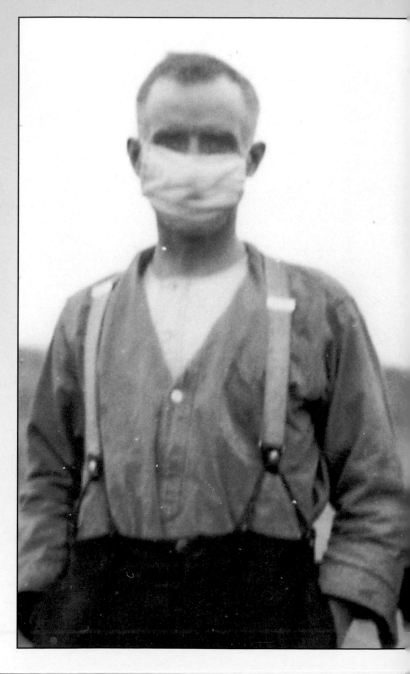

Of all the social changes that took place during the turbulent 1920s, none was more apparent than the discarding of Victorian and Edwardian attitudes to women's fashion. Gone were traditional ankle-length dresses and long hair, replaced by the rising hemlines and bobbed hair that became known as the "flapper" style. Popularized by the new movies, the short, loose dresses and cropped hair of the flapper became emblematic of the modern woman of the Jazz Age. The more daring, like Medicine Hat's Beatrice Broberg (centre in this photograph), even incorporated the style into their wedding dresses. Many older Canadians were shocked by such developments, which of course made them even more popular.

The Roaring Years

An Impatient Generation
Chases The Canadian Dream

I fear all that can be hoped for is a partial recovery of the religious instinct, and with it of home life, such as will abate the craze for hustle and bustle.

Professor Maurice Hutton

The Canada which emerged from the Great War was very different from the country that had entered the conflict in 1914, bursting with naive enthusiasm and certain that the boys would be home by Christmas. The adventure had turned into a murderous, gruelling test of the abilities and determination of Canadians. The rock-solid Edwardian belief in God, King and the nobility of Empire had been badly shaken by the unspeakable slaughter, but in its place was a growing national self-awareness and self-confidence.

Sixty thousand Canadians had died in Europe and many more had been wounded; thousands of whom would never fully recover. As the country had taken on a larger and larger role in the fighting and in munitions and food production, the war had become Canada's first truly national experience, shared by citizens from coast to coast. The effort had tested the resources and resolve of the young nation, and the wounds inflicted by the war - social and political - had been deep, but out of the conflict came a greater sense of national identity than ever before and a growing confidence that Canadians could overcome any challenge.

Many if not most Canadians expected the sacrifices and achievements of the war to translate into improved job opportunities, greater prosperity and better living conditions. The generation that had been bloodied in Flanders was less patient than its forbears. Life, they had learned, could be fragile and fleeting. They wanted their piece of the Canadian Dream now, not tomorrow. The result was a new focus on materialism, entertainment and the raw, boisterous enjoyment of life. The decade following the war was lively, chaotic and marked by a quickening pace of social change. It was a time of shills and charlatans, of fads and fancies, always with an eye on making a buck.

For most, the quest for the good life depended on a decent job. Yet within days of the armistice the Imperial Munitions Board cancelled contracts, which resulted in almost 300,000 layoffs. By the summer of 1919 those looking for work were joined by 400,000 soldiers, sailors and airmen discharged from the armed forces. At the same time international demand for Canadian exports (which by now accounted for more than a third of the country's annual income) slumped and prices fell. In the U.S., Canada's largest market, the slowing economy prompted protectionist measures to save American jobs - which worsened conditions north of the border. Even wheat, the engine of the Canadian economy, suffered as prices dropped by more than 50 per cent.

The result was a recession, which lasted until the mid-1920s. Unemployment rose to around 15 per cent and real wages, in most cases, tumbled from their wartime highs. Although most skilled workers and tradesmen were still making considerably more than they had in 1914 - an income of $1,000 a year was now possible in Canada's larger cities - that had to be balanced against a whopping 60-per-cent increase in the cost of living.

The post-war years were particularly difficult for returning veterans, many of whom had been

Photos - National Archives of Canada

Returning troops march through Sault Ste. Marie, Ontario in 1919 (above), and Princess Patricia's Canadian Light Infantry parade outside Ottawa's Chateau Laurier Hotel (opposite page). Nearly 400,000 soldiers, sailors and airmen were soon looking for work in a post-war recession.

subjected to the most intense, horrific combat in history. Many felt they couldn't explain their experiences to those who had not been there. This made re-integration difficult - and, for some, impossible. These silent, wounded men became a fixture of post-war society - mute witnesses to the unspeakable.

The debt owed to the veterans was widely acknowledged. Across the country, in communities small and large, there sprang up no less than 1,300 war memorials or cenotaphs. They were a very public expression of the nation's grief, but also of its pride in the achievements of Canadians on the battlefield. An amazing 3,000 captured German artillery pieces were hauled all the way from Europe to grace memorials from Halifax to Whitehorse. And John McCrae's "In Flanders Fields" provided an enduring hymn of remembrance, not just in Canada but around the world. The blood red Flanders poppy, worn each year as the eleventh day of the eleventh month approached, would come to symbolize public respect for the sacrifice of men and women in uniform.

On the practical side, however, Canada had no experience in dealing with the needs of hundreds of thousands of returning veterans and the learning process was long and chaotic. The federal government quickly created the Department of Soldiers' Civil Re-establishment and a rudimentary

pension scheme. It also set about looking after the tens of thousands of seriously disabled, but it would be a dozen years before a full system of veterans' benefits was established. As a result, many vets set up their own support groups and in 1925 these united into a lobby group with real and lasting influence: the Royal Canadian Legion.

For a country of barely more than seven million people in 1914, Canada's contribution to the war, in soldiers and materiel, had been enormous (much greater, proportionally, than that of the United States) and the effort had altered its position on the world stage. The goal of greater independence from Britain and wider international recognition of Canada as a nation in its own right, which had seemed so distant in the Laurier years, had become an immediate reality. Most of Britain's leaders were aware that without the support of the Empire, and in particular Canada, the outcome of the war could have been quite different. The other dominions and colonies now increasingly looked to Canada to referee relations with the mother country.

Canada's contribution to the war effort had also raised its profile in Europe. For the first time

The turbulent post-war years seemed full of unanswered challenges. At the League of Nations assembly in Geneva, Switzerland (below), Canada's contributions to the war effort had earned the country a seat at the table. But could the politicians really outlaw war? At home a reinvigorated Liberal party, led by labour lawyer and economist William Lyon Mackenzie King (left in the photograph on the opposite page, en route to an Imperial Conference in London), offered fresh ideas and an end to social unrest. But could King actually deliver?

the country was seen as more than a colonial appendage of Britain. In the U.S. there remained a strong tendency to view Canada as "British North America" - particularly in government circles - but there was also recognition and respect for Canadian military achievements. The careless assumptions of 1911, when a number of American politicians and newspapers had argued that Canada must inevitably be absorbed by a mighty and expanding Union, were fading rapidly. Professional soldiers on both sides of the border continued to plan for invasion and defence, but the animosities of the 19th century were fading into history.

Prime Minister Robert Borden attended the peace conference convened in Paris at the beginning of 1919 and endorsed the Treaty of Versailles. It was the first time Canada had signed an international treaty on its own behalf. Strangely, Borden left the official signing to two of his ministers. He had expressed concerns that the harsh conditions imposed on the defeated Germans were neither practical nor wise. (Time would prove him right.) The Paris conference also created the League of Nations to promote international peace and stability, and Canada became a founding member.

The lofty goals of the League of Nations - a lasting peace and world harmony - proved difficult to achieve amid the chaos left by the war to end all wars. The conflict had swept away the ruling monarchies of Germany, Russia and the Austro-Hungarian Empire. Much of Europe was in economic and political turmoil, and in Russia there was civil war as the Bolsheviks attempted to impose a new and revolutionary order. It was inevitable that Canada, too, would feel the impact of this wave of political, economic and social change.

In the post-war years the spread of Russian-style revolution was seen by many politicians and business leaders as an immediate threat, and the class-war rhetoric of many labour leaders only exacerbated their fears. Labour reforms had begun, slowly, before the war, and during the conflict the Borden government had for the first time officially recognized the right to union membership and collective bargaining. The concessions had seemed necessary to guarantee production and labour peace during the wartime emergency. Now, however, they combined with radical ideology and the impatience for better times to create a volatile mix.

Photos - National Archives of Canada

Employment was not always what returning veterans had hoped for. The meat packing industry had helped pioneer modern production techniques (the Toronto plant above is processing hogs), but it was still terribly hard work. Nevertheless, life still had its simple pleasures. These youngsters (left) are off for an outing aboard the steamer *Elsie*, shown leaving Toronto harbour.

Before the war relatively few Canadians had belonged to unions, but American labour organizations in particular had become very active north of the border, recruiting tens of thousands of new members and boosting total union membership to about one in five non-agricultural workers (about 400,000). When the wartime ban on strikes was lifted in 1919 there was an immediate increase in labour unrest. Strikes erupted in all major cities as labour demands crashed headlong into the slowdown of the economy.

The conflict came to a head in Winnipeg in May 1919, when metal workers went on strike to protest their employers' refusal to negotiate improvements in wages and working conditions. When the Winnipeg Trades and Labour Council called for a general strike in support of the metal workers, the massive response caught employers and political leaders by surprise. Within a few days, virtually the entire labour force was off the job and the city ground to a halt.

The revolutionary bloodbath in Russia was fresh in many minds and there was some loose talk among strike leaders about the creation of "a new order." To skittish politicians it sounded like a call to insurrection. Winnipeg's business leaders and middle class responded by creating a Citizens' Committee, which saw "Bolsheviks" and foreign agitators at every turn. Even the leadership of the national Trades and Labour Congress was alarmed, with president Tom Moore describing the situation as "semi-revolutionary madness."

In the spring of 1919 Winnipeg seemed close to anarchy as public services were suspended and hundreds of protesters took to the streets. Moments after this photograph was taken, this streetcar was set ablaze.

City of Winnipeg Archives

With public services suspended and hundreds of protesters in the streets, the Manitoba capital seemed on the verge of anarchy. Sympathy strikes were occurring in other cities across the country. The federal, provincial and civic governments were persuaded that the Winnipeg situation represented an immediate threat to law and order and their own authority. The no-nonsense federal Interior minister, Arthur Meighen, ordered a heavy police and military presence to enforce the Riot Act and clamp down on demonstrations - even peaceful ones.

On June 21, in the most serious clash between police and strikers, one person was killed and

Ordered into the Manitoba capital by the federal government, troops are drawn up on the city's Main Street (below) on June 21, 1919. The violence that day, which became known as Bloody Saturday, brought the general strike to an abrupt halt.

30 injured as Mounties charged a crowd of demonstrators. Bloody Saturday, as it became known, shocked the city to its core. Public support for the strike crumbled and a week later it was all over. Several strike leaders were arrested and jailed (including social reformer J.S. Woodsworth), but attempts to convict them of sedition were unsuccessful - although several foreign-born "agitators" were deported.

The Winnipeg strike may be the most famous, but over the next several years, as the economic recession took hold, there were many more affecting all regions of the country and virtually all

industries. It would be years before the bitterness engendered by these disputes would fade, but in the short term they convinced many social reformers (Woodsworth among them) of the need for political alternatives to Canada's traditional two-party system. They were not alone in their disillusion. Regional grievances, demands for trade reform and in Quebec the lingering resentment over conscription had eroded support for both major federal parties. From the Maritimes to Alberta, the 1920s would be a decade of political protest movements and splinter parties.

The most organized and powerful of the new political groups were created by Canada's farmers. Many were still smarting over the defeat in 1911 of the free trade initiative with the U.S. and the Borden government's wartime about-face on the farmers' exemption from the draft. There were also the immigrant farmers who were still upset over being branded "enemy aliens" and who had been disenfranchised in the 1917 election.

The urbanization and industrialization of Canada had begun before the Great War, but picked up pace considerably in the years that followed it. These children (below) are shown picking potatoes on the family farm on Prince Edward Island, but many Canadians were now leaving the land in search of jobs at factories such as this one (right).

Photos - National Archives of Canada

Led by the Western Grain Growers Association and the Dominion Grange (the largest farmers' organization in Ontario), the farm lobby had been politically active before the war. (In 1910 a demonstration of 800 farmers had brought Ottawa to a standstill and helped convince Prime Minister Laurier to embrace free trade.) Protest had necessarily been muted during the war years, but with the return of peace the farmers once again began to flex their political muscle. Success came quickly, albeit often ahead of coherent policy or organization. The Ontario provincial election of 1919 was won by the United Farmers of Ontario, supported by members of the Independent Labour Party. Two years later the United Farmers of Alberta took power in that province, despite having no leader and no candidates in sixteen of the province's 61 constituencies. The farm lobby also effectively controlled the governments in Manitoba and Saskatchewan.

In 1919 the country was still governed by Borden's Unionist coalition, made up of Conservatives and pro-conscription Liberals. Cobbled together to deal with a wartime crisis, it was poorly equipped to deal with the challenges of a peacetime economy. It passed on an opportunity to implement limited tariff reductions on imported goods, which would have helped Canadian farmers reduce their costs at a time when crop prices were falling dramatically. That was the last straw for a group of western MPs in the Union government. Led by Manitoban

Thomas Crerar, a former head of the Western Grain Growers, they left the government to form the Progressive party. Crerar, an intelligent and thoughtful man, was a passionate economic reformer and saw free trade as the defining issue of the times. The Progressives rallied around a "New National Policy" which promised reduced protectionism and relief for the country's struggling farmers.

There was discontent in the Maritimes, too. The region had experienced some prosperity during the war years, and the larger cities had boomed. But with the post-war manufacturing slump, the region was pummelled by a sharp decline in demand for its coal and steel. The downturn also aggravated its traditional handicap: remoteness from the industrial heartland of North America. Cape Breton was hit by a series of violent labour disputes, which dragged on for four terrible years. Unemployment once again became a fixture of life and younger Maritimers resumed the traditional trek west in search of opportunities they could not find at home.

Yet despite a persistent lobbying effort, the region never managed to get Ottawa's full attention. It could have forged an effective alliance with the new provincial governments in the West,

This native farmer (below) sticks with traditional horsepower to plough on a Saskatchewan reserve in 1920, while a steam powered thresher (left) is used in harvesting at Perdue, Saskatchewan. The internal combustion engine would soon make both obsolete.

Photos - National Archives of Canada

which were also agitating for economic and political reforms. Instead the Maritimes, led by Nova Scotia, raised the ire of Saskatchewan and Alberta by opposing their control over natural resources - unless the older provinces were handsomely compensated for the loss of a "national asset."

In 1920 the Unionist caucus elected Meighen, a lawyer from Portage la Prairie, Manitoba, to replace the retiring Robert Borden. Smart but often stubborn and tactless, Meighen was thoroughly Edwardian in outlook and determined to return Canada to its pre-war bliss. Like Borden before him, he believed in modest government and was slow to react to post-war economic difficulties or complaints from West and East. Meighen had also drafted the Borden government's wartime conscription legislation, which was all most Quebeckers and many farmers needed to know about him.

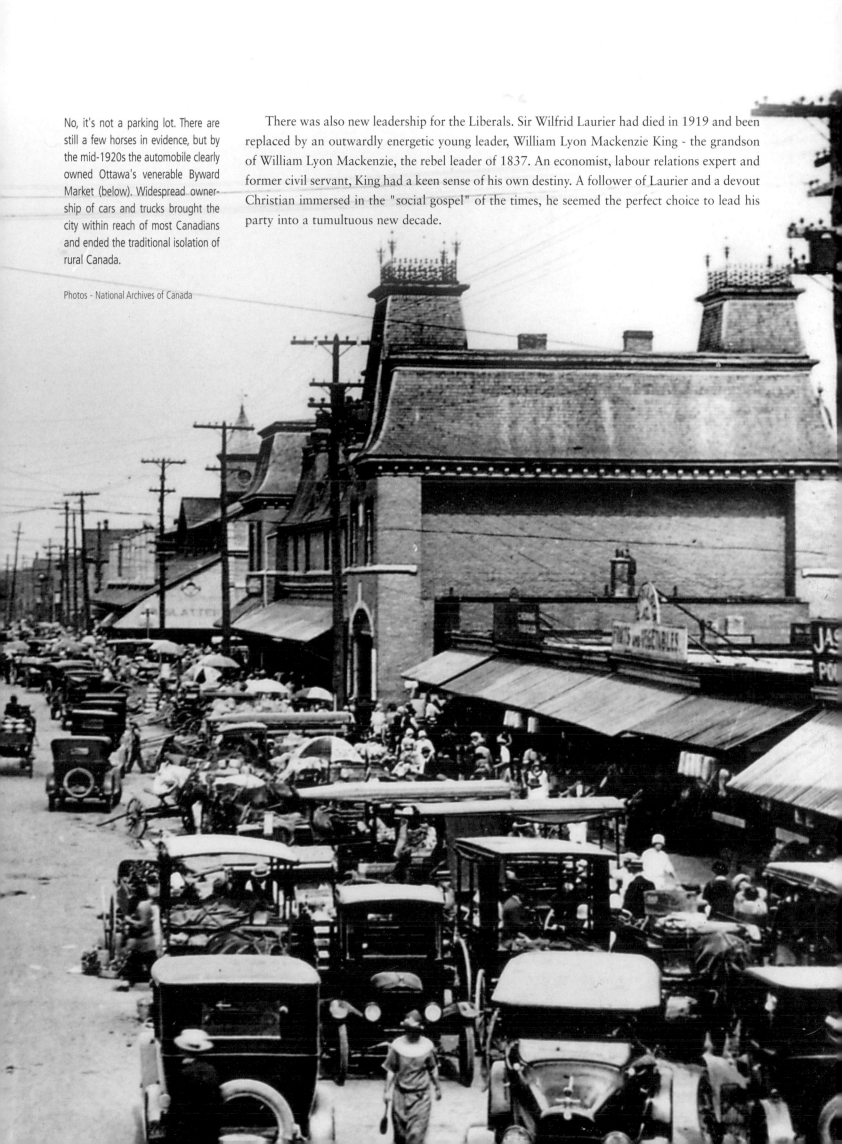

No, it's not a parking lot. There are still a few horses in evidence, but by the mid-1920s the automobile clearly owned Ottawa's venerable Byward Market (below). Widespread ownership of cars and trucks brought the city within reach of most Canadians and ended the traditional isolation of rural Canada.

Photos - National Archives of Canada

There was also new leadership for the Liberals. Sir Wilfrid Laurier had died in 1919 and been replaced by an outwardly energetic young leader, William Lyon Mackenzie King - the grandson of William Lyon Mackenzie, the rebel leader of 1837. An economist, labour relations expert and former civil servant, King had a keen sense of his own destiny. A follower of Laurier and a devout Christian immersed in the "social gospel" of the times, he seemed the perfect choice to lead his party into a tumultuous new decade.

A Royal Canadian In Mind And Spirit

In 1919 the Prince of Wales (later the Duke of Windsor) arrived in Canada for a cross-country royal tour. It's safe to say that no member of the royal family, before or since, has ever been such an instant hit. Sir Joseph Pope, who had organized the royal visit of 1901, was astonished by the public response to the prince. "I simply cannot understand what has come over the Canadian people," he wrote. "This utter lack of control - it is not at all what I would have expected." Unexpected or not, the prince became enamoured with the people and the country. "Although not actually Canadian born, I'm a Canadian in mind and spirit and come here as such - not as a stranger or a visitor," the prince wrote to his father, King George V. "And that goes down well." Indeed it did. He even bought a 4,000-acre ranch in the Highwood River valley, south of Calgary, "to find occasional escape from the sometimes too-confining, too-well-ordered island life of Great Britain." His marriage to American divorcee Wallis Simpson would later result in permanent exile from that life, but on this trip there was only sunshine. Enthusiastic crowds meet the prince in Nanaimo, B.C. (top right). Posing with two native guides during a hunting trip (bottom right). Duck hunting in Saskatchewan's Qu'Appelle Valley (below), and near Banff, Alberta, dressed in full regalia as Chief Morning Star of the Stoney Cree (left).

Photos - National Archives of Canada

The general dissatisfaction with the Unionist government found dramatic expression in the election of 1921. The coalition was reduced to 50 seats and third-party status behind the Liberals (with 116 seats, thanks to overwhelming support in Quebec) and Crerar's Progressives (64 seats in Ontario and the West). King had done a remarkable job of reuniting his party, but with barely 40 per cent of the popular vote it had too small a majority to govern with much authority or bring in sweeping reforms - which appeared to suit the new prime minister very well. As Canadians would come to appreciate, King was a very cautious man and, for a politician, strangely introverted. (It would be decades before the country discovered just how strange.)

The election of 1921 was typical of many throughout the century in demonstrating what separated Canadians rather than what united them. In Quebec the resurgence of the Liberals was welcomed as a sign that French Canada would once again "take her rightful place in government," while in Ontario the newspapers fretted about the rebounding influence of Quebec, Catholicism and western reformism. "The union of the regions is but partially accomplished," lamented the *Queen's Quarterly* magazine, while the *Canadian Forum* gloomily predicted that "No federation can prosper or even exist permanently" if the "sectionalism" apparent in the election results was allowed to fester. It was clear that national unity - Goldwin Smith's "Canadian question" of 1886 and Wilfrid Laurier's "supreme issue" at the turn of the century - was still very much at the heart of Canadian affairs.

For the next four years King governed with the precarious support of the Progressive caucus, which had declined the role of Official Opposition because, as a reform movement, it refused to do "politics as usual." Crerar's party ran the gamut from disaffected Ontario Liberals and social reformers like Agnes Macphail (the first woman elected to Parliament), to angry farmers from Ontario and Manitoba and their more radical cousins from Alberta. (The latter rejected the party system altogether, and often defied Crerar's leadership.) They were a varied bunch, but they all agreed that in Ottawa democracy was subordinate to vested interest, corruption and patronage. Parliament, they argued, represented the country Canada had been, not the country it now was, and needed reforming. These complaints would surface again and again throughout the century.

National Archives of Canada

William Lyon Mackenzie King (above) talking to delegates at the 1919 Liberal Party national convention in Ottawa, and campaigning in the 1921 federal election (opposite page). The result was a minority government for King, and many commentators worried about the disunity of the country and the fractured state of Canadian politics. It would not be the last time they worried about such things.

Taking To The Air

Canadians And Planes Seem Made For Each Other

ost Edwardians had been fascinated with the idea of airplanes. It was the practical aspects of powered flight they had problems with. Everyone knew how inherently dangerous it was, and what possible use could it be to the average person? It was, at best, a hobby for the wealthy and eccentric.

People like Alexander Graham Bell. The inventor of the telephone and sometime resident of Brantford, Ontario, had a summer home at Baddeck on Cape Breton Island where he founded the Aerial Experiment Association (AEA). For years Bell and a group of young aviation enthusiasts experimented with kites and balloons, and eventually built their first aircraft: the *Silver Dart*. On February 23, 1909, engineering student J.A.D. McCurdy piloted the plane to a height of 3 metres and kept it in the air for over a kilometre - much to the astonishment of a crowd of locals who had assembled to watch the fun. It was the first flight in Canada and the British Empire.

Bell and his young associates would continue to refine and improve their aircraft, and even tried to interest the federal government in its military potential as a bomber. The idea was dismissed as ludicrous.

National Archives of Canada

Despite Canada's enormous geography, and the fact the country had provided many of the top Allied pilots during the Great War, Ottawa was reluctant to create an air force. It wasn't until 1924 that the Royal Canadian Air Force came into existence. This photo (above), taken that year, shows the crew of an RCAF Vickers Viking flying boat at Victoria Beach, Manitoba. In 1927 the RCAF was trimmed to a headquarters and several training squadrons. Starved of funds and personnel, it would not function in a military sense until the outbreak of World War II.

Having developed a passion for flying, many Canadian pilots of the Great War were reluctant to be grounded. Among them was Bill Barker VC, one of Canada's top flying aces of the war, and later a business partner of another Canadian VC, Billy Bishop. This photograph (above) shows Barker in 1919 at the controls of a German Fokker D VII aircraft at the start of an air race between Toronto and New York. Ironically the plane had been captured during Barker's last dogfight. He went on to help found the RCAF, and was killed in a flying accident at Ottawa's Rockcliffe airfield in 1930.

Ottawa's disinterest in airplanes was still apparent two years into the Great War, when the government balked at creating a pilot training scheme in Canada for the Royal Flying Corps (the British air force of the time). It was left with little choice in the matter when a group of RFC officers arrived at Camp Borden, Ontario, and started training pilots. By the end of the war the RFC-Canada Program had trained over 3,000 Canadian pilots, about 2,500 of whom served in Europe or elsewhere overseas.

To ensure a supply of aircraft for the new fliers, the RFC also encouraged the building of an aircraft factory in Toronto. Ottawa eventually contributed $1 million to the start-up and within six months Canadian Aeroplanes, as the new business was called, had built 150 Curtiss JN4D planes (affectionately known as Jennys). Within a year the bustling plant employed 6,000 people and was turning out more planes than the RFC could use (as many as a dozen a day) and began selling them to the U.S. The aircraft industry had arrived in Canada.

One of the factors which had brought the RFC to Canada was recognition that Canadians seemed to have a particular aptitude for flying. Early in the war hundreds of Canadian volunteers had gone to Britain to train as pilots, while thousands more transferred to the RFC from the army. Clearly, Ottawa's lack of interest in flying was not shared by many young Canadians, who eventually accounted for a third (12,000) of all pilots who served in the RFC and the smaller Royal Naval Air Service (which amalgamated into the Royal Air Force in April 1918).

Many of the war's top flying aces were Canadian, led by Lieutenant-Colonel Billy Bishop of Owen Sound, Ontario, with his incredible 75 enemy aircraft destroyed; Nanaimo, B.C.'s Major Raymond Collishaw with 68; and Dauphin, Manitoba's Major Billy Barker with 58. (Barker won the Victoria Cross for single-handedly taking on 60 German aircraft, and shooting down five of them despite being wounded in both legs.)

Flying itself was not supposed to be difficult. One RFC instruc-

The legendary Katherine Stinson. Only the fourth woman in the United States to get her pilot's licence, Stinson (known as "The Flying Schoolgirl") delivered Edmonton's first air-mail in 1916 as a publicity stunt for the Edmonton Exhibition, She made the flight from Calgary to the Alberta capital in just over two hours.

tor described it as "a little easier than riding a horse," but the fact that 6,000 pilots were killed or seriously injured in accidents during the war years suggests it was considerably more dangerous than that. The planes were new technology, quirky at best and unreliable at worst, but for some the lure was irresistible. Better pay, no mud or trenches and lots of glamour.

Author H.G. Wells wrote of air combat, "No legendary feats of the past, no battle with dragons or monstrous beasts, no quests that man had hitherto attempted can compare with this adventure in terror, danger and splendour." The splendour came with a hefty price tag. The death toll among pilots was the highest of any arm of military service, and by war's end almost 8,000 British pilots had been killed in action, a quarter of them young Canadians.

Yet after the war the pool of trained airmen, mechanics and surplus planes would have a profound impact on the future of aviation in Canada. Some pilots, well and truly bitten by the aviation bug, would find ways to continue flying and make a living in the air. Renowned wartime flyers like Don MacLaren (a founder of Trans-Canada Airlines), Roy Brown (credited with shooting down the fabled German ace, Manfred von Richthofen), and "bush pilots" Freddie McCall and Wilfrid "Wop" May helped glamourize and legitimize civil aviation.

In the process they brought air travel into the mainstream of Canadian life, improving transport, communications and bringing even the most remote areas of the North within their reach. As the railways had done a generation earlier, civil aviation would shrink the distances which separated Canadians and help unify the country in the process. ■

The Western Canada Airways office, at Hudson, Ontario, in December 1926. As the railways had done a generation earlier, these pioneers of the air would shrink Canada's huge distances and end the isolation of the northland.

The modified Vickers Vimy bomber of Capt. John Alcock and Lt. Arthur Whitten Brown being checked over at Lester's Field airfield near St. John's, Newfoundland. The pair took off from St. John's on June 14, 1919 - and 16 hours and 27 minutes later landed at Clifden, Ireland. It was the first non-stop aerial crossing of the Atlantic.

The inauguration of Canadian airmail service at Montreal in 1928. Unofficial air mail service had been going on between various Canadian locations (and between Vancouver and Seattle) for more than a decade, but with so much money invested in the railways Ottawa had been reluctant to endorse a competing service.

The notion of Canada adopting a higher international profile as a result of its wartime efforts was quickly forgotten. The country was a member of the new League of Nations but otherwise avoided international entanglements, and Mackenzie King rejected Robert Borden's pursuit of more influence within the Empire. With influence came obligations, which King preferred to avoid. He returned to Laurier's goal of full political independence. Canada would decide if and when it would support the mother country.

It was a policy not always appreciated in London, where it sometimes appeared that Canada wanted to have its cake and eat it too. The issue came to a head in 1922 when King refused a clumsy request by Britain's new Colonial Secretary, Winston Churchill, to send Canadian troops to a strategic Mediterranean outpost at Chanak on the Dardanelles, where a British garrison had been surrounded by an army of the new Turkish republic. (Churchill, assuming Canada's participation, had informed the press of his request before informing Ottawa.)

London saw Chanak as critical to preserving the post-war status quo in the Eastern Mediterranean and international access to the Black Sea. King saw it as a dangerous leftover from the war and a presumption of automatic Canadian support for British foreign policy, and wanted nothing to do with it.

Despite such differences most British leaders understood that the war had made full political independence for the Dominions (Canada, Australia, New Zealand and South Africa) inevitable.

Pilots returning to Canada after the Great War found innovative ways to keep flying, including offering joy rides and taking photographs from the air. The new perspective on familiar scenery was an instant hit, and the thousands of aerial photographs of the period constitute a unique record of a changing country. This photograph of Brockville, Ontario (right) was taken in 1920. The twin cantilever bridges over the Niagara River (below) were captured for posterity in 1919. And this unusual photograph (left), taken that same year, shows a captured German submarine on display in Toronto.

Photos - National Archives of Canada

Most likely it would evolve along the lines suggested by Robert Borden in 1917: self-governing nations "of an Imperial commonwealth." Even the royal family was coming to the same conclusion. During his visit to Canada in the summer of 1919, the Prince of Wales (the ill-fated future Edward VIII) observed that "the Dominions appreciate being put on the same level as the U.K.... They've done so much to pull the Empire out of the war victoriously that one must recognize their established status as self-governing states of the Empire."

These were difficult years for Britain. The Great War marked a quantum shift of power to the United States. Britain had entered the war with the most powerful navy in the world and leader of the strongest economic bloc representing the world's largest source of capital. By 1918 that situation

Canadian Pacific's *Empress of Canada* (below) setting out in 1922 on her maiden voyage from Vancouver to Japan, China, and Hong Kong. Known as the "Queen of the Pacific", she was the first significant addition to CP's fleet after the Great War, and the first CP ship to offer an around-the-world-cruise (in 1924). The magnificent liner was converted to a troop ship during World War II, and in March 1943 she was torpedoed in the South Atlantic by an Italian submarine and sank in 20 minutes. Ironically, most of the 392 people killed were Italian prisoners of war.

had been dramatically reversed. The cost of the war to Britain went far beyond its one million dead, with the most lasting impact to be found in high finance and on the high seas. Britain ended the war a net debtor, its greatest obligations owed to the U.S., but perhaps the clearest indicator of the shift in global influence was that the Royal Navy, for the first time in more than a century, was forced to share its dominance of the oceans. In the Caribbean and Pacific it would increasingly be America and not Britannia which ruled the waves.

The Edwardian years had been the high-water mark of Empire, although many in Britain were loathe to admit it. Novelist Sir Arthur Conan Doyle was typical when, during a 1923 visit to Canada, he wrote: "Everywhere there is a consciousness of the glory of the Empire, its magnificent future, and the wonderful possibilities of these great nations all growing up under the same

flag with the same language and destinies. This sentiment joins with material advantages, and will prevent Canada from having any aspiration towards [full] independence." A decade earlier he might have been right, but the world was changing and the Empire and Canada with it.

The dreadful bloodletting of the Great War had fatally wounded the widespread and almost mythical belief in the nobility of the Empire. The carnage had decimated an entire generation in a poorly managed and essentially futile war, and the bonds of Empire had been forever loosened. Whatever meaning Canadians brought home from the battlefields of France, whatever rationalization they could find for the awful slaughter, came from the achievements and growing maturity of their own country.

The open observation car of a Canadian Pacific Railway train near Field, B.C., in 1924. Despite the economic and social upheavals of the 20s, middle class Canadians were travelling more and more. The Canadian Rockies had become an international destination, drawing well-heeled visitors from Europe and the U.S. - including the new breed of movie stars.

National Archives of Canada

Hockey Nights In Canada

A National Obsession Gives Birth To The NHL

The origins of ice hockey are obscure and still hotly debated. In fact, no one can say for certain where, when, or why Canadians first took to the ice to chase a puck, but by the end of the 19th century there were already scores of amateur teams playing hockey in communities across the country in a dozen different leagues.

This explosion of interest in the game had its roots in the mining, logging and farming towns which sprang up during the 1880s and '90s. There were few recreational opportunities in these often isolated communities, but two things never in short supply were young men and winter. Employers were quick to sponsor teams and help build facilities. As one manager explained, it was "much better than leaving the lads idle."

In 1892 Lord Stanley became the first Canadian governor general to lend his name to a national sports trophy; this one for the championship of the Amateur Hockey Association of Canada. Originally called the Dominion Hockey Challenge Cup, Lord Stanley's mug would survive into the 21st century as the Holy Grail of professional hockey.

The game also began attracting money. In the cities, top "amateurs" could earn as much as $1,800 a season, and even on less prosperous teams it was common for players to find a cash "donation"

tucked into their skates before the start of a game. By 1911 the National Hockey Association, the Canadian Hockey Association and the Pacific Coast Hockey Association had developed into quasi-professional leagues. Players such as Art Ross, Newsy Lalonde, Bert Lindsay, Cyclone Taylor and Georges Vezina were household names. Taylor signed with Renfrew (Ont.) of the NHA for $400 a game ($5,000 a season), which was more than the Detroit Tigers paid Ty Cobb, the number one player in baseball!

The Great War hurt the developing sport by taking away players and fans, but in a curious twist it also led to the formation of what would become professional hockey's dominant league. In the 1916-17 season, the NHA awarded a franchise to an army unit, the 228th Battalion, the Northern Fusiliers. The 228th played for several months (in khaki-coloured uniforms, naturally), but by February the battalion was ordered overseas. The subsequent attempt to restructure the NHA schedule created a major rift between Toronto Arenas' owner Eddie Livingstone and the league's four other teams. Unable to settle their differences, the NHA was dissolved - to be reborn in November 1917 as the National Hockey League.

The original NHL included the Ottawa Senators, Quebec Bulldogs, Montreal Canadiens, Montreal Wanderers and the Toronto

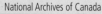

Pick me, pick me! Boys choosing sides for a hockey game on Sarnia Bay, Ontario (above), in the winter of 1908. Canada's national passion was already well established.

Arenas - minus their fractious former owner, Eddie Livingstone. The NHL's first season was hardly a sign of great things to come. The Bulldogs couldn't put together a team, attendance was abysmal and midway through the season the Wanderers dropped out after fire destroyed the Montreal Arena. (The more determined Canadiens, who shared the facility, moved to a smaller rink and played on.)

The game was also prospering out West. With a large wad of cash from the sale of the family lumber company, and with impressive new arenas in Victoria and Vancouver, Frank and Lester Patrick's Pacific Coast League was thriving. Encouraged by the PCL's example, in 1921 a group of prairie hockey entrepreneurs founded the Western Canada Hockey League, with franchises in Calgary, Edmonton, Regina and Saskatoon. The two western leagues would link schedules and eventually merge into the Western Hockey League.

The NHL, meanwhile, had overcome its early troubles and gone from strength to strength under the energetic leadership of a new president, Frank Calder. In 1925 he announced ambitious plans for expansion into Boston, New York and Pittsburgh (which the following year, with the addition of Chicago and Detroit, would become a five-team American Division). The move rapidly consolidated the NHL's position as hockey's premier league and franchise fees soared from $15,000 to $50,000. That same year - the 1924-25 season - the WHL's Victoria Cougars would be the last non-NHL team to claim the Stanley Cup. The following season most of the Cougar's top players decamped to Detroit to form the nucleus of the new NHL club there.

In New York, Rangers' manager Conn Smythe found himself at a loose end after being fired by owner Colonel John Hammond. Bankrolled with money he won gambling (reputedly $160,000), Smythe left for Toronto where he bought into a new NHL ownership group. Full of patriotic fervour and certain of hockey's future as Canada's game, they named their new team the Maple Leafs. ■

The first recorded women's hockey game took place in 1892 in Barrie, Ontario. The encyclopaedia of the NHL places the first official contest in Ottawa, in 1899. By the turn of the century women's hockey teams were playing across Canada (the photo above was taken in 1903). Female participation in Canada's game would eventually wane, only to be revived towards the end of the century. The New York Americans of the NHL (below), finished as runners-up in the league in the 1928-29 season, and the successful expansion into the U.S. ensured the NHL's future as the premier hockey league.

Prime Minister King and Canada's delegates at the 1926 Imperial Conference in London. (Left to right) Ernest Lapointe, King, Vincent Massey, and Peter Larkin. Lapointe was minister of justice, and Larkin (founder of the Salada tea company) was Canada's High Commissioner in London. Massey had just become Canada's first ambassador to Washington, and the conference sounded the death knell for Britain's control of Canadian foreign policy.

The Canadian desire for political independence was by now unstoppable. It would lead, in 1926, to the Balfour Declaration, which defined a new relationship between Britain and the Dominions. Heavily influenced by the cautious Canadian PM, the declaration confirmed Canada to be "autonomous" (rather than independent) but "in no way subordinate" to the government in London. Half a dozen years later the Statute of Westminster enshrined the country's full political independence into law.

In this changing world it was clear that Canada also needed to carefully reposition its relationship with its neighbour and increasingly powerful major trading partner. Mackenzie King understood this. He had spent most of the war years in the U.S. working for industrialist John D. Rockefeller (conveniently avoiding the question of military service) and was well connected in Washington. As prime minister he was determined to do nothing to upset the growing trade between Canada and its southern neighbour.

By 1926 the U.S. had replaced Britain as Canada's main source of foreign investment, but perhaps more important was the form that investment took. Rather than the more conservative bonds through which British investors had financed the early development of Canada's railways, mines and man-

ufacturing industries, the Americans often preferred riskier direct investment and ownership. Their keen interest in Canada's potential would have the effect of drawing the country into an ever closer relationship with its southern neighbour, and become the defining characteristic of Canada's economic development.

In domestic affairs, despite high public expectations there was little to distinguish Mackenzie King's first term in office. The overall impression was that the new government didn't do very much.

St. James Street, Montreal, in 1920 (above). Montreal remained Canada's largest city, but the 1921 census confirmed that Ontario now had more people than Quebec. The provincial government in Quebec City demanded a recount.

Tuna fishermen (below) at Hubbards, Nova Scotia, in 1928. Canada's traditional industries were flourishing, fuelled by a rapid growth of exports to the U.S. By the late 1920s the U.S. had replaced Britain as Canada's main source of investment and major economic partner. American investment and ownership would have a profound impact on the development of the Canadian economy through the 20th century.

It addressed some minor concerns over freight rates and subsidies, and under pressure from social reformers in the Liberal and Progressive ranks, it had introduced a limited old age pension (for those over 70 who could show they were virtually destitute). But beyond that, King tinkered, modified... and did little of anything beyond directing government building projects to Liberal constituencies. Above all he avoided any issue which, like conscription, might divide both the country and his party.

In the House of Commons Prime Minister King was continually unsettled by the dogged Arthur Meighen. The pair had known each other since their student days at the University of Toronto and their loathing was mutual. "As soon as Meighen stood up to speak, one could note from the gallery the prime minister's sudden congelation," King biographer Bruce Hutchison wrote in *The Incredible Canadian* (Longmans, Toronto, 1952). "A line of scarlet rose slowly up the back of his neck until it flooded his bald scalp. As Meighen, erect, gestureless and glacial, poured on the vituperation, King oozed pure hatred." Their mutual animosity would frame Canadian politics for two decades, but while Meighen was an accomplished orator who could make King squirm in Parliamentary debate, the dumpy, unprepossessing prime minister was more than his match when it came to political strategy and an understanding of the Canadian voter. He was not, though, infallible.

King called an election in 1925 in an optimistic frame of mind, expecting to make gains at the expense of the disorganized and unfocused Progressives. This he did, regaining a number of seats for the Liberals in the Prairie provinces, but the big surprise was the resurgence of the Conservatives. When the votes were in, the Tories led with 116 seats to 101 for the Liberals and 25 for the Progressives. Rather than resign as prime minister, King decided to hang on to power with the support of the Progressives - who disliked the Tories rather more than they disliked the Grits.

The alliance between the business-as-usual Liberals and the Progressive reformers was an uneasy one, not helped by the fact the Liberals quickly became embroiled in a major scandal involving the Customs Department. In the summer of 1926, faced with looming defeat in the

Canadian National's transcontinental train "The Confederation" crossing a bridge at Lytton, B.C. (below). Tying the country together with steel had been an enormously costly undertaking, but by the 1920s few people doubted the value of what Wilfrid Laurier had termed "nation building."

Even as late as the 1920s, some of Canada's more remote communities still had the look and feel of frontier towns. The photograph above shows Main Street, Kirkland Lake, Ontario, in 1927. The utility poles and automobiles can't mask the rugged nature of the town.

Commons, King went to Governor General Viscount Byng (former commander of the Canadian Corps at Vimy) and asked him to dissolve Parliament and call a new election. Byng refused. Since no party had won a majority in the previous year's vote, he had given King the opportunity to govern and was determined to give Meighen and the Tories the same opportunity. It was a decision which would trigger one of the strangest crises in Canadian politics, and sadly tarnish the reputation of a war hero and an honourable representative of the Crown.

Asking Meighen to form a government was an option quite within Byng's power under the constitution. The Tories had, after all, won the most seats in the 1925 election. In addition, Byng felt he'd given King fair warning that if the Liberal-Progressive coalition fell apart, Meighen would be given a chance to govern. King didn't see it that way. He had governed for more than half a year, so he felt the governor general was obliged to call an election if he asked for one. He branded Byng's decision high-handed imperialism. Meighen, of course, jumped at the opportunity offered by the governor general. But his government soon faced a Parliamentary challenge to its legality, which the Tories lost by a single vote, finally forcing an election.

The campaign set a new low for cynicism. While Meighen tried to focus on Liberal corruption and limp trade policy, King made the election a referendum on independence from Britain: A titled Englishman had hijacked the legitimate government of Canada! "We have reached a condition in this country," he claimed, "that threatens the constitutional liberty, freedom and right in all parts of the world." The idea that the Tories and the hero of Vimy were somehow intent on rolling back Canadian independence, which had been paid for in blood on the battlefields of Flanders, was nonsense, but it worked. After the votes were counted King and the Liberals were back, with a majority this time, and the crestfallen Meighen was soon replaced as Tory leader by wealthy Calgary lawyer and entrepreneur Richard B. Bennett.

A roadside picnic near Locust Hill, Ontario, in the spring of 1927. With more speed than the vehicles themselves often could muster, during the 1920s the automobile rapidly became a fixture of Canadian life. Distances were no longer measured in miles, but in the time it took to drive.

46·334

The Automobile

Noisy, Unreliable, And Dangerous
The Future Arrives On Solid Tires

There were but a handful of the new automobiles in Canada in 1905, and none being built here, when young Sam McLaughlin wheeled a two-cylinder American Buick into his father's carriage-making business in Oshawa, Ontario.

At the time most people were convinced the noisy, unreliable and manifestly unsafe automobile had little future - including McLaughlin's father: The McLaughlin Carriage Company advertisements used images of wrecked and broken-down automobiles to promote the safety and reliability of horse-drawn transport. But the younger McLaughlin worked to mate the Buick engine with a more sturdy carriage of his own design, and in eighteen months had created the first Canadian-built car.

At the time there were no gas stations and few highways, but within a remarkably few years Canadians were buying cars in enormous numbers. The Great War helped spur the mass production of all manner of vehicles, from trucks to motorcycles, and the technology rapidly became more reliable and less expensive. By 1920 Canada was even an automobile exporter. Foreign car and truck sales totalled $18 million; more than the combined value of Canadian wheat and flour exports barely a decade and a half earlier!

Regulations governing the operation of motor vehicles were minimal. Drivers' licences weren't required in most cases, and driver training usually consisted of a few minutes' instruction from a salesman. Accidents were common, but rarely fatal in an age when twenty miles per hour was considered a very respectable speed.

The train had already made day trips and recreational travel a possibility for many city dwellers (particularly in southern Ontario and the Montreal area), but it was the automobile which would truly revolutionize Canadian travel habits. You could visit relatives, see the sights - and just as the automobile made the city more accessible to the country, the country became more accessible to city folk.

Glenbow Archives

An increasingly mobile population began to routinely think of distances in terms of how long it took to drive somewhere. The price of gasoline became as familiar a topic of conversation as the price of bread and milk, and new fortunes were made in the manufacture and sale of automobiles and the fuel to run them. One such was Charles Trudeau, the father of a future prime minister, who developed a chain of gas stations in and around Montreal.

No other innovation of the 20th century, not even television or the computer, would have a greater impact on the lives of ordinary Canadians; alter patterns of work, leisure and even courtship; change the very look of the urban and rural landscape. North America's embrace of the automobile would also deepen the cultural divide between the New and Old Worlds. Restricted by a more conservative culture, shorter distances and an older urban landscape, it would be another 40 years before automobile ownership would become commonplace in most of Europe, and it would never root quite as deeply in European attitudes and lifestyles. ∎

National Archives of Canada

Canada's love affair with the automobile outran the ability of governments to build roads for the suddenly mobile population. Outside the major cities (and very often within them) mud and ruts were the order of the day, which took its toll on the vehicles (opposite page). But if all else failed you could call the early equivalent of a tow truck (below) to get you moving again. The demand for cars and trucks had actually begun before the Great War (the photo above shows a Willy's Overland dealership in Galt, Ontario, in 1915). By 1920 there were 400,000 registered motor vehicles in Canada, and that number would increase to more than a million by the end of the decade.

National Archives of Canada

Canada passed its first federal highways act in 1919, and within a decade some 130,000 kilometres of paved highways had been laid - plus hundreds of thousands of kilometres of gravel and dirt roads. The idea of combining camping with driving was an early innovation (immediate left, and below). A not-so-welcome development was traffic congestion. This early example of a traffic jam (opposite page, top) was photographed on Toronto's Sunnyside Drive in 1926.

Photos - National Archives of Canada

The Grey Cup

Hip Flasks And Frozen Turf
Create A National Institution

When Governor General Lord Albert Henry George Grey decided to sponsor a national championship trophy for Canadian sport, his first thought was of the game which was already becoming the nation's abiding passion: hockey. But hockey was already taken. His predecessor, Lord Stanley, and Montreal millionaire Sir H. Montagu Allan had both donated hockey trophies.

Earl Grey was nonetheless determined to have his name on a cup and, as a product of England's public school system, he would have been familiar with the game of rugby football. So his second choice was the game's Canadian cousin.

The first contest for what would become known simply as the Grey Cup was an all-Toronto game. On December 4, 1909, the University of Toronto defeated the Toronto Parkdales 26-6 in front of a boisterous crowd of about 4,000. A contemporary report noted that hip flasks and fur coats were required to stave off the wintry chill. A Canadian institution had been born.

Well, almost. The University team had to wait until the following March to actually receive the $48 trophy. Apparently someone on the earl's staff had forgotten to place the order with Birks Jewellers.

The first East-West final took place in 1921, again in Toronto, when the Edmonton Eskimos challenged the Argonauts for the cup - and received a 23-0 drubbing at the hands of the local team. Canada's Athlete of the Half Century, the legendary Lionel Conacher, scored 15 of Toronto's points before leaving the field at the end of the third quarter. Conacher wasn't injured. He had to lace on his skates to play hockey that same evening.

Fired by such exploits, football's popularity grew rapidly during the 1920s and the importance of the Grey Cup game grew with it. The cup final would eventually become bigger than the game itself, taking on mythical status as a forum for East-West rivalry and an alcohol-fuelled national bacchanal. The league would endure some very tough times, but the championship game always seemed to revive it. It also ensured that, in Canada at least, the Grey family would be remembered for something other than the second earl's favourite blend of tea. ∎

The Hamilton Tigers football club in 1906 (below). When Earl Grey, the governor general, couldn't sponsor a championship trophy for Canadian men's hockey, he turned instead to a game with solidly British roots - football - and created an enduring institution that, often against the odds, survived and prospered beyond the 20th century.

In February 1922, Canadians were shocked to discover that the previous summer's Sixth Decennial National Census had pegged the country's population at 8,888,483 - well short of the expected ten million. People had become so used to the idea of rapid population growth that there was widespread consternation and public comment when Dominion Statistician R.H. Coats reported that Canada's population had grown less rapidly between 1911 and 1921 than it had during the previous decade. Even taking into account the war and the Spanish influenza epidemic, many people viewed a 1.5-million increase over ten years as decidedly subpar for a country which was destined to own the 20th century.

The news was taken particularly hard in the West, where many community leaders had confidently predicted the population would double in each decade. Many sceptical westerners were not surprised when four enumerators in Regina were arrested and charged with falsifying returns - but it turned out they had been padding the numbers, not underestimating them. In Quebec there was suspicion that Coats had underreported the province's population (2.3 million compared to Ontario at 2.6 million) for political reasons. An indignant government in Quebec City immediately moved to set up its own provincial census bureau.

But not only were the numbers accurate, they really were very positive considering the Great War had seriously disrupted the flow of immigrants from Europe for four years. As Coats pointed out in a flurry of press releases, Canada's percentage growth from 1911 to 1921 (22 per cent) had been better than the U.S. and globally it had been second only to Australia. His explanations were accepted, somewhat reluctantly. The *Calgary Herald* offered a typical response: "Canada would be disappointed in the census returns, were it not that the last decade has been decidedly unfavourable for large increase in population. In the circumstances, the showing the Dominion

J.W. Miller's thriving hemp crop (below), near North Battleford, Saskatchewan, in 1920. Some envisioned great things for the versatile marijuana plant, but it's safe to say no one would have predicted that eight decades later it would be at the heart of a multi-billion-dollar illegal drug trade.

Provincial Archives of Alberta

Through the work of artists such as the Group of Seven's Tom Thomson (above) and Emily Carr (right), in the 1920s Canada for the first time began to recognize a distinctive culture all its own. The Group of Seven became internationally acclaimed after an exhibition of their work in London in 1924.

has made is not unsatisfactory."

There was, in fact, much to learn from the census. It confirmed the continuing westward flow of population. Saskatchewan now had the highest per capita income in the country, and the Prairie provinces and B.C. were now home to 30 per cent of Canadians, compared to 10 per cent in the Atlantic provinces-a complete reversal of the picture a mere twenty years earlier. Almost 100,000 people had left the Maritimes for the West, the U.S. or the cities of central Canada. In a single decade, Nova Scotia had fallen from Canada's third most populous province to its seventh.

The census confirmed Ontario and Quebec as home to a majority of Canadians (60 per cent), but perhaps the most striking statistic was that, for the first time in the country's history, as many Canadians now lived in towns and cities as in the country. Montreal was still the largest city, with 618,000 people, but Toronto (at 521,000) was quickly gaining. Winnipeg (179,000), Vancouver (163,000), Hamilton (114,000) and Ottawa (107,000) had all crossed the six-figure threshold. Montreal and Toronto together were now home to more Canadians than all three Maritime provinces combined. The new cities of Saskatchewan and Alberta were smaller, but considering that 25 years earlier they had been little more than frontier outposts their growth had been spectacular. Edmonton's population had reached 58,000, Calgary 56,000, Regina 34,000 and Saskatoon 25,000.

In 1921 the number of native-born Canadians was also higher than ever before (77 per cent). Of every 1,000 Canadians, 515 were male (only Argentina had a more masculine society), and an astonishing 43.5 per cent of Canadians were under 20 - while only 15 per cent were over 50. Immigration had made up the losses from the war, and seen to it that Canada remained decidedly male and predominantly young.

French Canadians and those of British ancestry still dominated the country's ethnic makeup, although as a result of immigration francophones had fallen to 27.9 per cent of the total population - in spite of Quebec's astonishing birthrate. More than 55 per cent of Canadians claimed English, Irish, Scots or Welsh roots. Canadians of German origin (3.3 per cent) made up the largest group which was neither British nor French, while Canadians of Ukrainian descent (1.3 per cent) had moved into a fourth-place tie with those of Dutch origin. The actual number of Ukrainian Canadians was almost certainly under-reported, since many still gave their origin as Russian or Austrian, depending on who had governed the part of Ukraine they had emigrated from. The fact that the census forms consistently misspelled "Ukranian" likely hadn't helped matters.

The census also revealed some important truths about life in the Twenties: Despite the political unrest and the increasing pace of social change, underneath it all Canada remained a conservative society rooted in its Victorian and Edwardian traditions of family and faith. Among those between the ages of 35 and 50 an overwhelming 80 per cent were married. The country also had the lowest divorce rate in the Western world. (Manitoba had recorded its first ever divorce in 1919.) Fully 97.6 per cent of Canadians identified themselves as Christian. In fact, out of a population of 8.8 million, a miniscule 22,000 reported no religious affiliation. At 3.3 million, Roman Catholics made up 40 per cent of Canada's Christians, with most of the rest spread between the Presbyterian, Anglican and Methodist churches. Yet Catholics were a majority only in Quebec. Among other faiths, Canada's growing Jewish population (125,000) was by far the most numerous.

The youthful demographics and the popularity of marriage had a clear impact on the national birthrate, which was a healthy 29.3 live births per thousand population. Quebec's birth rate of 37.6 was, according to the Dominion Bureau of Statistics, "the highest rate of natural increase" in any jurisdiction where reliable statistics were kept. Advances in medical science and more emphasis on public health were enabling more children to survive into adulthood. Dr. Alan Brown of Toronto, an early pioneer in the field of pediatrics, invented Pablum and in 1923 published the first popular modern Canadian guide to parenting: *The Normal Child: Its Care and Feeding*.

Between the ages of 5 and 18, 61 per cent of Canadian children were in school (up from barely more than 50 per cent in the 1911 census), and the average student could expect to receive 8.5

years of education. Secondary schooling had, by now, become a fixture in most provinces. In Ontario, schooling was compulsory for all children to the age of 16. The Prairie provinces, B.C., Nova Scotia and Prince Edward Island all let children leave school at slightly younger ages, but they had followed Ontario's lead in dropping most fees for secondary education and were more vigorously enforcing their truancy laws. In New Brunswick, children were still allowed to leave school at age 12 and many did, while in Quebec education remained the responsibility of the church (Catholic and Protestant) and school attendance remained a matter of parental choice. Post-secondary education was still a rarity in Canada in 1921, with less than 50,000 people enrolled in the country's 23 universities (many still new and small) and various colleges.

The 1920s were chaotic, difficult years with uncertain markets for traditional Canadian exports, but in an age of astonishing technological change there were other opportunities. New industries appeared to manufacture automobiles, radios, telephones and domestic appliances such as the washing machine, vacuum cleaner and refrigerator - made possible by the spread of electricity and indoor plumbing to most homes in Canada's towns and cities. It would be a generation or more before these things were as common in rural Canada (by the end of the decade only one in ten farms had electricity), but the growing demand for power, water, communications and roads also helped diversify the Canadian economy, provide new jobs and offset the lacklustre international demand for the country's natural resources.

The signing of the federal-provincial agreement on old-age pensions (below), in Ottawa on May 18, 1928. Great War veterans had previously been awarded limited pensions, but this was the first "universal" social program to be cautiously endorsed by the King government. It seemed affordable, since only 15% of the population was over 50.

National Archives of Canada

National Archives of Canada

The Canadian delegation to the League of Nations (above) at Geneva, Switzerland, September 1928. Membership had been a prime goal of Prime Minister Robert Borden after the Great War, but by the late 20s it was apparent Canadian involvement was more an issue of status than collective security. In the words of Senator Raoul Dandurand (third from the left), Canada lived "in a fireproof house far from inflammable materials."

There were developments in transport and communications, which would have a profound impact on the still largely undeveloped country. The innovation which would most shape this new Canada was the automobile. In 1914 there had been 74,000 motor vehicles registered across the country. The year after the war ended there were 342,000, of which 60 per cent were privately owned passenger vehicles. Within a decade the number of privately owned vehicles would climb to over a million, in a country of barely seven million people.

The result was a revolution in transportation. The train had conquered Canada's vast distances and allowed the country to begin to tap its vast resources for export. But at the local level, travel in much of Canada had remained difficult and time-consuming. By horse and buggy a trip of 20 miles was an all-day affair, and for the millions of Canadians who lived in the country a visit to the city was anything but routine. The car and truck would change all that, shrinking travel times and the very perception of distance. And with the expanding highway system came electricity, telephones and access to urban conveniences and markets. Modern Canada was taking shape.

The post-war years also saw the beginnings of a revolution in entertainment. Previous generations had either made their own entertainment at home or supported communal efforts (such as choirs and amateur theatrical groups): Only in the larger towns and cities had there been the occasional opportunity to see professional performers. Now phonograph recordings, radio and the silent movies made it possible for performers to reach an audience of millions. As technology improved and entrepreneurs explored the business possibilities of the new entertainment media, costs came down and public interest soared. By 1920, the electronic media had become firmly entrenched in popular culture.

Women In Politics

The Famous Five Become Persons

The Great War and the Christian social reform movement helped sweep away many of the barriers which had restricted the involvement of Canadian women in politics. In the Alberta provincial election of 1917, temperance campaigner Louise McKinney and nursing sister Roberta MacAdams became the first women elected to any Canadian legislature. The first woman elected to the Parliament of Canada was Agnes Macphail, a teacher from Grey County, Ontario, who ran as a Progressive in the 1921 election.

Ironically, it is not the election of these pioneering female politicians and others in the immediate post-war period which is most remembered or revered by later generations, but rather an argument over the admission of women to the un-elected Canadian Senate: An institution with a reputation, even then, as a sinkhole of political patronage rather than a bulwark of democracy.

Section 24 of the British North America Act limited Senate membership to "persons" and, in a traditional interpretation which clearly ran counter to the reformist mood of the times, women were deemed ineligible. This bastion of male privilege was famously challenged by five Alberta women who had already made their mark in public life; Nellie McClung, a writer, political activist and former MLA; Emily Murphy, the first female magistrate in the British Empire; Irene Parlby, an MLA and cabinet minister; Henrietta Muir Edwards, a founder of the Victorian Order of Nurses and the National Council of Women; and politician Louise McKinney.

In 1928 the Supreme Court of Canada rejected an appeal by the "famous five" and confirmed that women were not "persons" for the purposes of Senate membership. The following year the case was heard by the Judicial Committee of Britain's Privy Council, which at that time was the final court of appeal in the Empire. This venerable institution of the monarchy decided that the exclusion of women from the Canadian Senate was "a relic of days more barbaric than ours."

As a result of the judicial victory it was widely assumed that Judge Murphy (or Nellie McClung, a good Liberal and former politician) might be the first woman appointed to the Senate, but in what was surely an intentional slight Prime Minister Mackenzie King appointed instead Cairine Wilson, a veteran Liberal party organizer, as Canada's first female senator. Prime ministerial prerogative was preserved.

Agnes Macphail would serve as an MP until 1940, help found the Co-operative Commonwealth Federation (the forerunner of the New Democratic Party) and later serve in the Ontario Legislature for another decade. Yet despite the growing involvement of women in political life and their enormous influence on public issues there were relatively few female MPs and provincial legislators until the 1960s, when a "second wave" of Canadian feminists would plunge into professional politics. ∎

In 1921 Agnes MacPhail (above) became the first woman elected to the House of Commons. Writer, social activist, and politician Nellie McClung (below), a good Liberal who Prime Minister Mackenzie King considered "a bit too sensational" to sit in the Senate.

Photos - National Archives of Canada

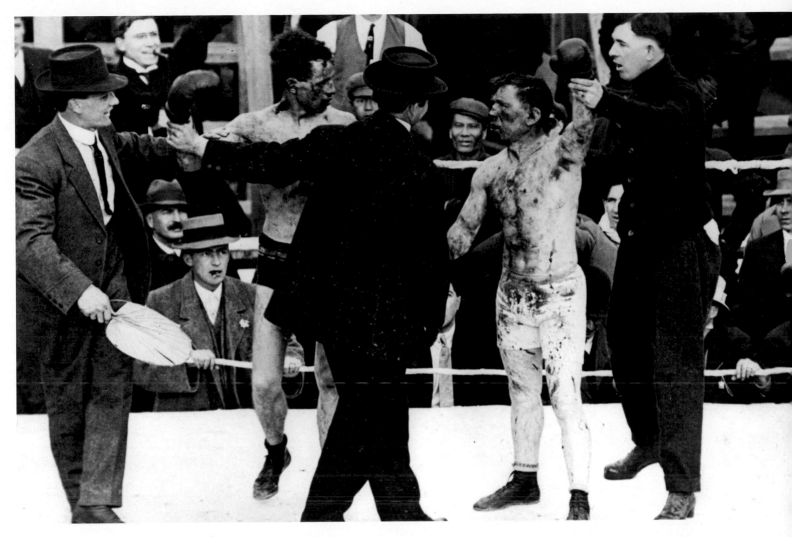

In what was obviously a bloody affair, two boxers (above) named Campbell and Hyland after a bout staged in Vancouver in 1913. Boxing, professional and amateur, was enormously popular, and not yet subject to the stringent controls of later years.

The movies were already predominantly American, produced by a rapidly growing industry in the Los Angeles suburbs, but from the very beginning Canadians such as Toronto's Mary Pickford (the first international superstar of the silver screen) found success in Hollywood and legions of fans at home. In the space of a decade, the movies went from being an unscripted, unprofessional and rather seedy alternative to legitimate theatre to the dominant form of mass entertainment. It was a multi-million dollar industry built on a voracious (and very un-Edwardian) public appetite for glitz, glamour and celebrity.

Radio was just as revolutionary in broadcasting entertainment, but with it also came the ability to instantly relay news and information from far-away places. For the first time most Canadians could hear the voices of the famous and the influential. But to a very large extent those voices were American. The Americans were, as usual, first to recognize the potential of the new medium. They built large, powerful transmitters that spilled U.S. broadcasts into Canada, filling Canadian homes with American politics, sports and music to an extent that had never before been possible. A *Toronto Telegram* poll in 1925 discovered that seventeen of the top twenty radio stations listened to by Canadians were American, sparking fears for cultural autonomy and the first demands for regulations and subsidies to foster the development of a domestic communications industry.

Torontonian Ted Rogers, for one, needed no help competing in the new market. He built more efficient receivers using alternating current and his Rogers-Majestic Company rapidly became the Canadian leader in the burgeoning radio industry. Despite ups and downs in a turbulent business not noted for longevity, the company would survive through the century as a fami-

National Archives of Canada

The temperance movement had been active in Canada since the late 19th century, but with the onset of wartime austerity, and the growing influence of women in public policy, prohibition became a major issue. Above, Toronto barmen parade along the city's Yonge Street to protest prohibition.

ly business and a leader in a Canadian home entertainment industry it helped to pioneer. By Canada Day, 1927 - the nation's Diamond Jubilee - a makeshift national radio network of 23 stations was able to broadcast the celebrations in Ottawa from coast to coast.

Alongside the fascination with new forms of entertainment, the early decades of the 20th century were marked by an astonishingly vibrant and successful Canadian literary scene and publishing sector. There were dozens of publishing houses, and books by and about Canadians sold in the millions. Stephen Leacock, Lucy Maud Montgomery and Ralph Connor (the pen name of the Rev. Charles Gordon) were international stars, and even authors writing for the domestic market like Nellie McClung could sell as many as 100,000 copies of their books. Nor was there any attempt to Americanize or internationalize Canadian content for foreign consumption. Canada was seen as an exotic, adventurous and even glamorous setting.

The new appreciation for things Canadian extended to the landscape, which most people had previously viewed as a challenge to be overcome or a barrier to the development of valuable resources. That had begun to change by the spring of 1920, when a group of seven young Toronto artists (six of whom had worked together as graphic designers) held an exhibition at the city's Art Gallery. Their unorthodox paintings of the Northern Ontario bush, full of vibrant reds, yellows, oranges and blues, shocked an art world which was not used to the idea of Canadians as artistic

Lights, Camera, Action!

Toronto's Gladys Smith
Becomes America's Sweetheart

The "moving picture" industry introduced the modern concept of celebrity to North American culture. And the first larger-than-life superstar of the silver screen was a diminutive Canadian.

Gladys Marie Smith was born at 211 University Avenue in Toronto on April 9, 1893. As Mary Pickford she would become the first in a long, long line of Canadian entertainers to head south in search of fame and fortune. She would also become the most recognized face in history, the most powerful woman in the new movie capital of Hollywood and the owner of a massive US$50 million personal fortune.

Gladys was the eldest child of John and Charlotte Smith. The family lived in the genteel poverty typical of a late-Victorian middle-class family trying to make ends meet in the global depression of the 1890s. John Smith tried a number of business ventures before buying a modest but profitable candy and fruit concession on the steamship *Chicora*, one of many plying Lake Ontario. The family seemed set - until Smith hit his head on a steel pulley aboard ship (legend has it that alcohol was involved). He at first appeared to recover, but a year later died of a blood clot caused by the injury.

For the surviving Smiths, life became very tough. "A bit of financial anxiety in childhood isn't a bad thing, as long as plenty of love goes with it," Gladys remembered in later years. "It's likely to give a person an extra drive and ambition." It certainly did in her case. When she was about 5, her mother reluctantly agreed to take in boarders, including the stage manager of the Cummings Stock Company: A theatre company producing a melodrama at the Toronto Opera House. He persuaded Charlotte Smith to allow Gladys and her younger sister, Lottie, to appear as extras for the

Mary Pickford in 1921. The little girl from University Avenue had become the most recognizable face in the world.

National Archives of Canada

then-substantial sum of $20 a week. From that point on little Gladys would be the family's main breadwinner, forsaking education (she had a total of six months' formal schooling) in favour of making a living.

By 1901 the whole family (Gladys, her mother, sister and younger brother) was touring the Eastern U.S. in various productions, with "Baby Gladys" as the star and the other three Smiths in supporting roles. Theatre had become the family business. Five years later, 13-year-old Gladys got her first Broadway role, but the producer demanded she change her name to something more glamorous. She combined her own middle name (Marie) and her great-grandmother's maiden name to come up with Mary Pickford.

In 1909, lured by the promise of $5 a day, Pickford took temporary work at Biograph, a New York movie company founded in 1895 by Thomas Edison's assistant, William Dickson. There were no scripts and everything from costumes to scenery and makeup were improvised. These silent films were screened mostly in converted stores, fitted with old train or streetcar seats.

To Pickford it seemed far less glamorous than the traditional stage, but there were hints of the potential bonanza to come. Tickets were only 5 or 10 cents, yet the movies could be mass-produced and there were already upwards of 12,000 "nickelodeons" across North America, with more opening every week. Movies which cost hundreds of dollars to make could return many thousands in earnings.

In 1914, Pickford's new employer, Famous Players, released her first big movie; *Hearts Adrift*. Her name was given top billing on nickelodeon marquees across the continent, which had never been done for an actor before. Her next film, *Tess of the Storm Country* was even more successful, and her salary was hiked to an unheard-of $2,000 a week. The next year it was doubled and the press began calling Pickford "the highest paid woman in the world," which she undoubtedly was.

Always careful with a dollar, Pickford had a businesswoman's mind. She and her sister would sometimes stand outside movie theatres and count the number of people going to see her films, to use as leverage in contract negotiations. It worked. Within two years she had a deal guaranteeing her $10,000 a week, half the profits from her films and a $300,000 signing bonus. She had become not just the highest paid woman, but the highest paid entertainer in the world. Famous Players even agreed to pay her mother (who was also her manager) $150,000 a year as a sign of "good will."

For the next decade and a half Mary Pickford would be the world's biggest celebrity, rivalled only by Charlie Chaplin. Thomas Edison christened her "America's Sweetheart" and the nickname stuck. Her fairytale marriage to actor Douglas Fairbanks (they actually married three times) and their lavish lifestyle helped create the extravagant and alluring aura of Hollywood.

In 1919, at the age of 26, Pickford, Fairbanks, Chaplin and director D.W. Griffiths founded their own company, United Artists, and confirmed their place at the pinnacle of the movie industry. Pickford now had power as well as wealth. In a career spanning 24 years, she acted in and produced more than 200 movies and in 1929 won an Oscar for her first sound picture, *Coquette*. She retired in 1932 after making only her fourth "talkie." Her legions of fans were stunned, but (like Wayne Gretzky more than six decades later) she explained that her reasoning was simple: "I wanted to retire at my peak."

Pickford remained a Hollywood icon until well into the 1960s and was a regular visitor to her hometown, but as time went on she became more and more reclusive, rarely appearing in public. She died in Los Angeles in 1979 at the age of 87. Thanks to her curious habit of buying up the rights to her own films and taking them out of circulation, she is less familiar to later generations than, say, Chaplin. Yet the girl from University Avenue with the trademark ringlets retains her place as the movie industry's first and perhaps greatest international star. ■

National Archives of Canada

Mary Pickford and Douglas Fairbanks at radio station CKAC in Montreal, 1922. The original Hollywood couple, they epitomized glamour and wealth.

Toronto police arresting a man for illegal possession of alcohol (above). In most of Canada prohibition burned itself out within a few years, but it left a lasting legacy in the form of government control of liquor sales and the forbidding government liquor store - a uniquely Canadian institution.

pioneers. *Toronto Star* art critic H.F. Gadsby labelled the paintings "hot mush," and *Saturday Night* reviewer Hector Charlesworth dismissed the group as mere "paint slingers."

But no artists before or since have captured the public imagination the way this group did. In a shot at traditional European painting, one of the seven, A.Y. Jackson, challenged Canadians to "replace the Dutch cow with the northern bull moose" in their appreciation of art. And they did. In the years following the Toronto exhibition the group became nationally famous and painted all parts of the country. Then, in 1924, a display of their work at the British Empire Exhibition in London won rave reviews. One critic called it "the most vital group of paintings produced since the war indeed this century." The Group of Seven had become an international hit.

The world of art and entertainment may have been celebrating non-conformity, but in other ways post-war society was hostile to individual freedom. By 1918 every province apart from Quebec had voted to outlaw the sale and consumption of alcohol. That same year the federal government had outlawed the manufacture and import of any beverage with an alcohol content above 2.5 per cent.

National Archives of Canada

By 1918 every province except Quebec banned the sale and consumption of alcohol. Not that everyone obeyed the rules. This photograph (above) shows a man carrying a keg of beer through the streets of Toronto.

The temperance movement had been active since the late 19th century, but the growing political influence of women and wartime austerity made prohibition more appealing. Supporters pointed to plummeting crime statistics as proof of its beneficial effects, but the lack of criminal activity likely had more to do with the fact that 650,000 young men were in uniform and otherwise occupied. In any event, prohibition in Canada was short-lived and not very successful. Canadian distilleries were allowed to legally produce liquor for export (mostly to the U.S.) - and a surprising amount of it found its way back across the border to eager consumers.

The federal prohibition laws were increasingly ignored after the war ended and within a decade only Prince Edward Island would cling to temperance legislation. Prohibition did, however, produce one distinctly Canadian institution: the government liquor store. Booze made its return as a very profitable provincial monopoly, but politics demanded that the sale of alcohol by the government could not be seen to imply either approval or enjoyment. Far from it. The government liquor store would be a stark and forbidding place, which fairly oozed condemnation of the sad individuals standing in line to fill out order forms.

Provincial "liquor control boards" now also governed the private sale and consumption of alcohol and official ambivalence to the demon drink was all-pervasive. The typical Canadian beer parlour became a place of anti-conviviality and very serious drinking. Temperance may have been a short-lived phenomenon, but it would be six decades before puritanical Canadian governments would countenance the forbidden delights of the neighbourhood pub or the debilitating influence of the wine bar.

Prohibition wasn't the only area in which Canadian women were exercising new-found influence. The temperance movement acted as a training ground for the first generation of female political activists. The war years had greatly accelerated the involvement of women in the workplace; they now made up almost 20 per cent of the labour force. And since they were disproportionately concentrated in the teaching and nursing professions, women naturally began to play a significant role in the social reform movements which argued for better public health and education.

When the world didn't end as a result of the growing involvement of women in public life, the arguments against enfranchising women rapidly began to crumble. Female property owners had been voting in most municipal elections since the late 19th century, and by 1917 they could vote in provincial elections in the Prairie provinces, Ontario and British Columbia. That same year the Borden government for the first time gave some women the right to vote in the national election if they were the mothers or wives of men in uniform. It was a self-serving move (the vast majority of women voted for conscription and Borden's coalition), but once it was done there was no going back.

In 1918 the Borden government extended the right to vote in federal elections to virtually all Canadians over the age of 21. By 1922 the Atlantic provinces had followed suit, but in Quebec there remained hostility to giving voting rights to what one well-known journalist termed "thousands of bird brains." Henri Bourassa, journalist, Liberal politician and ardent Quebec nationalist, warned

Prime Minster King signing the Multilateral Treaty for the Renunciation of War (below), in Paris, on August 27, 1928. Banning war was a bold but ultimately meaningless gesture, and a little more than a decade later peaceful Canada would find itself embroiled in another world conflict.

that giving women the vote would produce "the woman-man, a hybrid and dreadful monster that would kill the woman-mother and the woman-wife." It would be another eighteen years before women were allowed to vote in Quebec's provincial elections.

Influenced by the movies and the growing emancipation of women, the style of the1920s will be forever associated with rising hemlines, dance music and the "flapper" mystique. It represented a clear break with the more restrained (in public at least) Victorian and Edwardian eras and was as shocking to many older Canadians as the 1960s would be to a later generation. The Roaring Twenties are often dismissed as a flippant and superficial decade, yet the revolution in social mores, entertainment and the growing participation of women in public life represented a significant shift in the life of the country - and nowhere more so than in the workplace.

It seemed that no sooner had Canadians learned to drive than they wanted to see just how fast the new automobiles could go. Racing quickly became a popular spectator sport. These cars (below) are roaring around a track at the Central Canada Exhibition at Ottawa in 1925.

National Archives of Canada

By the early 1920s almost two thirds of the teachers in Canada's rapidly expanding education system were women, and for the first time women were graduating as doctors, lawyers and even a few as engineers. In less than a decade the number of female university graduates had grown from almost none to around 20 per cent of the total. Hundreds of thousands of women found jobs as nurses, clerical workers, telephone operators and in the shops and offices of the growing service sector. The shortage of male labour during the war years had seen a huge increase in the number of women employed in Canada's factories, and although many were replaced by returning servicemen the demand was so great that a significant number of women continued to work

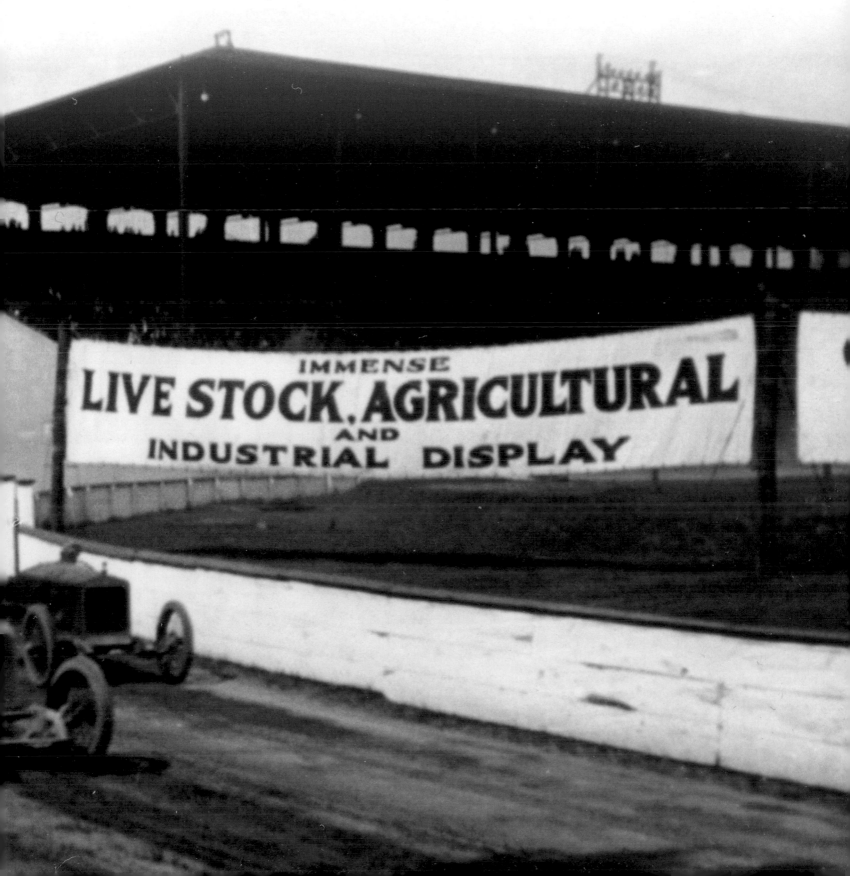

in manufacturing. Employment of servants - a traditional role for young women - was in decline, but many moderately well-off middle-class Canadians could still afford a maid and perhaps a cook, although it was now less common for them to "live in."

This new army of working women were mostly young, and (apart from teaching and nursing) the demands of married life and raising children usually meant a retreat from the workplace after a few years. But for the first time in history a large number of women now had some experience working outside the home for wages. Just as importantly, Canada was coming to rely on the additional labour, earnings and (not least of all) the tax-paying potential of women in the workforce.

For the first time, personal and corporate taxes were becoming a significant source of revenue for the Canadian government. The war had driven Ottawa deeply into debt, which led to the introduction of a business-profits tax in 1916 - and a year later personal income tax. Income tax was justified as a temporary "conscription of wealth" to help offset the costs of war, and in the 1920s it still seemed little more than that. The rate was a modest four per cent, with no tax on the first $1,500 earned (the equivalent, roughly, to $18,000 in 2000).

Percy Williams of Vancouver (opposite, right) being held aloft after winning the men's 100 metres at the 1928 Olympic Games in Amsterdam, Holland. It was one of two golds for Williams (he also won the 200 metre race). The astonished Americans later invited Williams to a series of track meets in the U.S., hoping to prove his Olympic performance a fluke. He won 19 of the 21 races, and in 1930 set a world record for the 100 metres. At the same Games, Saskatchewan's Ethel Catherwood (left) won gold in the women's high jump, becoming the only Canadian woman ever to win individual gold in Olympic track and field competition. The five medals won by the Canadian women's team (two gold, two silver, and one bronze) helped make 1928 Canada's best ever performance at the Summer Games, finishing four overall.

In the first decades of the 20th century the Canadian government remained modest in size and scope. Duties on imported goods remained Ottawa's major source of revenue. There were increasing demands that government take more responsibility for the welfare and safety of citizens, but this was still most often done through regulation rather than direct intervention. Few, if any, Canadians at the time would have predicted that income redistribution - from citizen to citizen and region to region - would become the federal government's primary function. None would have believed them if they had.

Despite the growing liberalization of society and the social gospel, the prevailing view among Canadians remained that individuals were ultimately responsible for their own welfare and that of their families. Churches and charitable organizations were the source of most assistance for those in difficulties, and even that help came with the very clear understanding that it was temporary. The idea that citizens were entitled to financial benefits from the state was still very radical. One exception was the new system of pensions finally put in place to help disabled veterans of the war. They were modest, but represented the first time Canadians as a society had offered ongoing financial assistance to a large group of fellow citizens.

The early years of the decade had been tough, with low prices, high unemployment and

Fritz Businski and his family (below) at their farm near Durban, Manitoba, in 1928. The Businskis emigrated from East Prussia after the Great War. The conflict had slowed the flow of migrants to Canada, but it picked up pace again after the armistice. Despite the war, there was surprisingly little animosity towards immigrants from Germany.

National Archives of Canada

Members of the Imperial Council of the Ku Klux Klan (above) with a Union flag at Vancouver in 1925. A KKK rally in North Vancouver that year attracted 500 people, and for a brief period the Klan was able to expand its activities in Montreal, Toronto, and particularly in Saskatchewan. Within a decade, though, it had all but disappeared from Canada.

even bank failures, but the vitality of the pre-war years had never been entirely extinguished. In the second half of the 1920s there was a noticeable improvement in the economy as demand for Canadian exports increased (particularly in the U.S.) and prices for everything from wheat to lumber to nickel rebounded.

On the international stage Canada seemed to be emerging from its post-war insularity. Between 1927 and 1929 the young country established its first embassies in Washington, Paris and Tokyo, and in 1928 the first British High Commissioner (ambassador) was appointed to Ottawa in recognition of the country's de facto independence.

In an effort to avoid opposition from ardent imperialists (still a powerful lobby), the King government modestly referred to these first embassies as "legations," but their establishment was nevertheless attacked by the Conservatives as "the end of our connection with the Empire." In Washington, the life of the first ambassador, Vincent Massey, was threatened by a distraught imperialist, but Massey's biggest problem was raising Canada' profile with the Americans, who tended to see his arrival as an unwanted complication of relations with the British Empire. When Massey presented his credentials to President Coolidge, the new ambassador was obliged to explain where, exactly, his hometown of Toronto was located. Washington was now, somewhat reluctantly, obliged to send its own representative to Ottawa. Coolidge wondered what, exactly, an American ambassador would do there?

Distributing Canadian-grown apples to British schoolchildren at the Imperial Fruit Show in Birmingham, England, in the fall of 1929. It's clear from the look of some of the children that hardship was already a feature of life in Britain, and was soon to become one for many Canadians. The Roaring Years were about to come to an end.

National Archives of Canada

Despite the lingering view in Washington of Canada as a backwater of the British Empire, the reality was that the 1920s had seen the emergence of a new nation north of the border. Canada's institutions were still overwhelmingly British, but with a distinctive North American egalitarianism which was increasingly different from the class-dominated attitudes of the old country.

Better transportation and communications had begun to shrink the country's daunting geography and bind a diverse people together. If the foundations of a national identity had been poured during the Great War, the walls were built in the Twenties. By the end of the decade, a majority of Canadians considered themselves something more than a junior branch of the global British family and something other than American. Defining that "something" was already becoming a national obsession.

Since 1900, Canada had become more urban, more diverse, and vastly more developed as agriculture opened up the West and industrial technology made it possible to harness more and more of the country's vast natural resources. The potential was there, the future still beckoned, and a good measure of the wonderful optimism of that first, golden decade of the 20th century had survived. During a visit to Canada in 1928, British statesman Ramsey MacDonald still sensed a country on the verge of greatness: "There are many reasons why I should like to live for one hundred years," he said. "One of the reasons is I would like to see this country one

The 1920s saw the first communications revolution, with radio providing instant entertainment and information in the home. It was a time of incredible innovation. In the photograph above, taken in Edmonton in 1922, the young man is wearing an early portable radio, with the receiver in a ring on his hand connected to a substantial earpiece. It didn't catch on - at least not until his grandchildren were adults.

hundred years from now. It will be great. It will be rich. It will be powerful."

And in a speech in Victoria in 1929, the noted Indian poet and philosopher Rabindranath Tagore praised the "incalculable potential" of the nation. "Her creative youth is still before her," he assured his audience. "Canada is too young to fall a victim to the malady of disillusionment and scepticism." And as the third decade of "Canada's century" drew to a close, there was little reason to doubt it.

With the economy rebounding, by 1929 there was a record 143,600 Canadians liable to pay federal income tax. That still represented only a small percentage of all income earners, but it was an indication of a growing middle class. The average wage had risen to $1,200 a year, although that was still significantly below the Department of Labour's estimate that a minimum of $1,430 a year was necessary to maintain a family of four. Money was still tight for the average Canadian, and after the purchase of necessities there wasn't a lot left over for entertainment or the new household gadgets coming on to the market. But the last half of the 1920s had finally seen an improvement in living standards to match the growing expectations of working people.

As prosperity rebounded some Canadians took note of the profits to be made in the stock

The Calgary head office of British Canadian Oils. The Canadian dream at 15 cents a share. Everyone wanted a piece of the action, and in the months before Wall Street crashed the Calgary Stock Exchange had to hire a night shift to keep up with public demand.

market - and there was no lack of promoters to help them find a sure thing. And why not? The difficult adjustments to a post-war economy seemed to have been made, the tough years were behind and the future looked assured. The middle class in both Canada and the United States eyed the swelling ranks of the wealthy and many decided they, too, deserved a piece of the action. In the late Twenties savings accounts were for the meek and unadventurous. The booming stock market was the place to make money.

The Calgary Stock Exchange was forced to hire night staff to keep up with market activity, and the city's brokerage offices were expanding by the week. The price of Home Oil Company shares went from $3.50 to $15.75 in the first two months of 1929, and that was modest growth compared to other oil companies. (Okalta Oil rocketed from $30 to $300 in the same period.) And it was the same story in Montreal, Toronto and Vancouver.

Understanding of the stock market was, however, minimal, as were regulations governing investment and trading. There was very little in the way of independent professional advice or unbiased business reporting - but just about everyone had a hot tip, a guaranteed winner. You could even buy on margin, putting no more than 5 or 10 per cent down. As long as business continued to expand and prices continued to rise you couldn't lose, and in 1929, as a new decade approached, Canada's captains of industry and finance were brimming with confidence. S.J. Moore, the president of the Bank of Nova Scotia, was typical

Banff National Park from Tunnel Mountain in October 1929. The challenges of the first three decades of the 20th century had gone a long way to forging a nation from a diverse country, and a revolution in transportation and communications had helped bring people and places closer together than ever before. In tune with the growing optimism of the times, on the brink of a new decade the president of the Bank of Nova Scotia confidently predicted "an unprecedented period of prosperity lies ahead." Unfortunately, the 1930s would prove him wrong.

National Archives of Canada

in predicting "an unprecedented period of prosperity lies ahead."

Few people gave much thought to the possibility that the stock market's bullish exuberance might be built on nothing more substantial than paper, and fewer still took much notice of the noise made by protectionists in the U.S. Congress and elsewhere. With hindsight, it's not difficult to understand why the generation which had survived the war, the Spanish flu and the unemployment and uncertainty of the post-war years wanted so desperately to believe the future would be as bright and prosperous as the first decade of the century had been for their parents.

Oh, a few curmudgeons suggested there would have to be a fiscal reckoning, including no less an authority than Cambridge economist John Maynard Keynes. But as the Roaring Twenties reached their crescendo, hardly anyone was listening. ■

About the Author

Veteran Alberta journalist, editor and author Paul Stanway writes a political column for *The Edmonton Sun* and other newspapers across Canada. His first book, *The Albertans*, was published by CanMedia in the spring of 2005 to coincide with the province's centennial. *The Albertans* went on to be a National best seller.

Paul was born in Manchester, England, and worked for several British newspapers before immigrating to Canada in 1976. He covered politics for *The Winnipeg Free Press*, before spending a year in Ottawa freelancing for the *The Toronto Sun* and other publications. He was a member of the start-up team that launched *The Edmonton Sun* in 1978, and served the paper in several senior positions before being appointed Editor of *The Calgary Sun* in 1988. In 1989 he was appointed European bureau chief and columnist for the Sun newspapers, based in London. He was appointed Editor in Chief of *The Edmonton Sun* in 1992, and left Sun Media in July 2001. In addition to his writing, he also works as an editorial consultant.

Photo and Archival Sources

The publisher gratefully acknowledges the generous assistance of the sources of the photographs and archival material contained in this volume: The National Archives of Canada, the Glenbow Museum and Archives, the Ontario Archives, the Manitoba Archives, Alberta Provincial Archives, British Columbia Archives, City of Toronto Archives, City of Vancouver Archives, University of Toronto Library, University of Manitoba Library, The Notman Archives (McCord Museum, McGill University), City of Edmonton Library, the Fort Garry Horse, Paul Stanway.

INDEX

Note: Numbers in italics refer to photographs or captions.

Toronto Island (ON), *124-125*
Toronto Maple Leafs (hockey), 273
Toronto Parkdales (football), 287
Toronto Star, 299
Toronto Telegram, 295
tourism and recreational travel, *112, 113, 270-271*
  camping*114-115, 257, 284-285*
  influence of automobile, *280-281, 282-283, 284, 285, 312-313*
  Rocky Mountains, *8, 312-313*
trade, 135, 276
  Canada-U.S. agreements, 38-41, 140
  free trade, 36, 41, 132, 140-142, 250-253
  tariffs, 22, 90, 152, 306
trade unions, 27, 153, 243, 245
trains. *See* railways
Trans-Canada Airlines (TCA), 262
transportation, 54
  transcontinental, *6-7*
  urban, *10, 16, 23, 86, 90, 92, 140*
  water, *12-13, 21*
  See also automobiles; railways; ships and shipping
treaties, *28-29, 77, 135, 301. See also* Versailles, Treaty of
Trudeau, Charles, 283
Truro (NS), 22
tuberculosis, *117*
Tupper, Sir Charles, 72-73
Turkey, 266

U
U-boats, 199, *266*
Ukraine and Ukrainians. *See* immigrants and immigration, Ukrainian
Union government, 152, 251, 253-254, 258
unions. *See* trade unions
Union of Soviet Socialist Republics (USSR), 228, *232*
United Artists, 298
United Empire Loyalists. *See* Empire Loyalists
United Farmers of Alberta (UFA), 251
United Farmers of Ontario (UFO), 251
United Kingdom. *See* Great Britain
United States
  American immigrants to Canada, 64, *62-63*
  annexation of Canada, 14-15, 16
  boundary disputes with Canada, 76-77
  Civil War, 14
  emigration to, *17, 20-22, 23, 29*
  Great War, 161, 206
  influence on Canadian culture, 295
  international influence, 77
  postwar, 269
  relations with Canada, 40-41, 140-142, 152, 243, 276, 307
  See also trade, Canada-U.S. agreements
University of Toronto, 68, 287
urbanization, 59, 84, 107, 112
utilities, public, *10, 27, 72, 92-95. See also* electricity

V
vaccination, 120-122
Valcartier (QC), *150, 155, 157, 175*
Vancouver (BC), 27, 77, *94-95,* 194, 273, *307*
  fires, 78, *83*
  population, 289
  railway, *6-7,* 29

See also Williams, Percy
Verdun (QC), *178-179*
Versailles, Treaty of (1919), 243
Vezina, Georges, 272
Victoria, Queen, 38, 73-74, 149
Victoria (BC), 27, 38, 81, 310
Victoria Cougars (hockey), 273
Victoria Cross, 45, 155, 212, 223, *261, 262*
Victorian Order of Nurses, 294
Victory Bonds, *200-201, 203*
Vimy Ridge (France), *185,* 186-191, *192, 193, 194, 233*
voting. *See* disenfranchisement; elections, federal; women, right to vote

W
Wallaceburg (ON), 173
wars. *See* Boer War; Great War; pacifism
Wartime Election Act (1917), 205
Washington (DC), 40
Webb, Sydney, 9
Welland Ship Canal (ON), *21*
Wells, H.G., 262
weapons and warfare, *160-161,* 173, *199*
  artillery, *158-159, 184-185, 204, 205*
  machine guns, *222, 226-227*
  innovations, 160, 194, *198, 204. See also* gas masks; Lee-Enfield gun; Ross rifle
West, Canadian, 29, 292, 301
  contribution to Boer War, 43
  hockey, 273
  influence, 258
  relation with Ottawa, 132-133, 152
  settlement, 25-29, *50,* 57-58, 61-63, 126
  See also Alberta; British Columbia; Manitoba; Saskatchewan
Western Canada Airways, *263*
Western Canada Hockey League, 273
Western Grain Growers Association (WGG), 250
Western Hockey League, 273
wheat
  export, 29, 64-65
  humour, 69
  prices, 53-54, 240
  varieties, 34, 68
Wilhelm II, Kaiser, 149
Williams, Maj. Victor A.S., *43*
Williams, Percy, *305*
Williams, Phyllis, *43*
Wilson, Cairine, 294
Windsor, Duke of. *See* Edward, Prince of Wales
Windsor, House of, 177
Winnie the Pooh, 175
Winnipeg, 26, *26, 27, 44, 93, 175*
  description, 67
  fires, *81*
  General Strike (1919), *236-237, 245-249*
  population, 65, 67, 289
  poverty, *98, 99*
  railways, 90
Winnipeg Trades and Labour Council, 245
Winona (ON), *118*
women
  employment, 120, 301, 303-304
  Great War, *176-179, 208, 218-219,*
  political activism, 119, 300-301
  right to vote (suffrage), 153,, 301
  sports, *273, 304*

Woodstock (ON), 95, *180-181*
Woodsworth, J.S., 249, 250
World War I. *See* Great War
World War II, 194, *269*

X, Y, Z
York, Duke and Duchess of (George V and Queen Mary), *74, 75*
York (ON), *90*
Ypres (France), 162, 166-171, 194
Yukon, *38, 53, 77*